MW01592756

PRAISE FOR TEAM COVENANT

"Randy Hopkins understands the new generation of employees and what they need in order to produce exceptional work. Team Covenant offers a thoughtful, holistic approach to human resources that puts people first."

—Daniel H. Pink, *NY Times* best-selling author of *DRIVE*

"We owe a special thank you to Randy Hopkins and Team Excellence who taught us how to build an organization. The Team Covenant has become the foundation of our company's culture and the basis upon which we work successfully together."

—Terry Andrus, President, CompleteRx

"For 12 plus years, Randy Hopkins has been our moral compass in the operation of our business. The understanding he has taught us about managing our people and the philosophy behind the Team Covenant are important guidelines that we live by daily."

—Richard Fant, CEO, New Process Steel, LP

"Our task was to reorganize our 105-year-old, outdated culture into a contemporary, streamlined and efficient business model. In the last three years, the Team Covenant and the Team Development Strategy have provided us the platform and process to dramatically transform our workforce from a keep-their-heads-down entitlement mentality into an engaged culture of accountability and highly motivated people."

—Thomas Gordon, COO, Catholic Extension

"The Team Covenant and Team Development Strategy have become integral to our culture and the way our managers and employees work together. Team Excellence provides us with a metrics-driven system along with a realistic definition and statement of our business philosophy that makes practical sense for our approach to performance management."

—Edward Griffin, President, Griffin Partners Inc.

"The Team Covenant and Team Development Strategy (TDS) have consistently exceeded our expectations in helping us build, cultivate and sustain a collaborative employee culture focused on bottom line results. TDS gives us the tools to define performance requirements within a system of measurable individual accountability. The Personal Strengths Inventory (PSI) especially has been a major contributor to achieving a greater level of employee engagement."

—Ruthie Lee-Esene, Human Resource Director, The BTS Team

"Over the past 25 years in the talent management business, we've used numerous traditional as well as more recent, online assessments, with a wide range of satisfaction and desired results. The PSI (core Team Covenant component), however, has risen to the top to be not only the most straightforward, focused and career-relevant instrument that we have used, but also does not require lengthy, ongoing certification processes for staff and consultants. It is cost-effective, expertly-created and of the highest psychometric and technological caliber - the overall best instrument we've found."

—Carolyn L. Greco, President, FACET

"It is with great appreciation that we offer our endorsement and support for Randy Hopkins and the Team Excellence "team" for their wonderful support and valuable insights into building, maintaining and developing teams of high achievers. Over the last 4 years, we have applied the "Personal Strengths Inventory" (PSI) and the team profile facility in a wide range of cultural environments, levels of education and various linguistic groups throughout Asia and the Middle East."

—Don Power, Managing Director, Power+ Executive Evolution

"Randy Hopkins and Team Excellence have provided us with the outstanding tool they call the Personal Strengths Inventory (PSI). This assessment tool is very simple for our clients to understand and has been invaluable to me and our team when working with executive teambuilding sessions and when providing individual executive coaching. The PSI is an integral part of our work as we assist in making individuals and organizations more effective. Randy Hopkins has done an outstanding job in making PSI and other Team Excellence tools very easy for consultants and clients to utilize and understand."

—Lonnie Bane, Principal Consultant, hrQ

TEAM COVENANT

An Award-Winning Employee and Organizational
"*Contract*" to Build Trust, Relationships and
Continuous Performance Improvement

all the best!

Randy Hopkins

RANDY HOPKINS

Copyright © 2012 by Randy Hopkins.

Library of Congress Control Number: 2012918960
ISBN: Hardcover   978-1-4797-3153-4
                    Softcover   978-1-4797-3152-7
                    eBook   978-1-4797-3154-1

All rights reserved. The materials in this book are provided for the personal use of the purchaser of this book. No redesign, editing, reproduction, or creations of a derivative work from these materials are permitted without the written permission from Team Excellence Inc. No part of this book may be used or reproduced in any manner whatsoever, including but not limited to, electronic, mechanical, photocopying, recording, or otherwise, without written permission except for the inclusion of quotations in a review.

The instructions and advice in this book are not intended as a substitute for psychological counseling. The author and publisher disclaim any responsibility or liability resulting from actions advocated or discussed in this book.

In the interest of preserving client confidentiality, some client names and, in some cases, identifying characteristics have been changed. The scenarios, situations, and results are real.

The Team Covenant™ and Team Development Strategy™ are trademarks of Team Excellence Inc.
http://www.teamexcellence.com

ATTENTION: For information regarding the use of the Team Development Strategy within your organization, or interest in having Mr. Hopkins speak to your organization, please contact: Team Excellence Inc., 1700 Post Oak Boulevard, 2 BLVD Place, Suite 600, Houston, Texas 77056 or send e-mail to info@teamexcellence.com.

This book was printed in the United States of America.

Rev. date: 07/31/2014

To order additional copies of this book, contact:
Xlibris LLC
1-888-795-4274
www.Xlibris.com
Orders@Xlibris.com
597972

To my friend, Ian, who brought his family to America to chase the dream. This book is dedicated to him and to his extraordinary passion for self-reliance and individual responsibility.
He continues to inspire me.

CONTENTS

ACKNOWLEDGMENTS

Thanks first of all to my wife, Carolyn, who has helped me, supported me, and encouraged me throughout the long developing journey of the Team Covenant. Her love, understanding, and generous caring nature have taught me the true meaning and importance of relationships.

I also want to thank staff and colleagues who have contributed so much to the clarity in presenting the Team Covenant story and, by doing so, ensuring that the book is true to our experiences. I particularly want to thank Karen Masullo for her intelligent and experienced insight and suggestions and to Eileen Hempel for her years of dedicated assistance to me. Also, my genuine appreciation goes to Pete Gerardo for his creative editing and transitional help that at times got me off dead center.

For his consistent commitment and programming brilliance, I can never thank Tom Allison enough for the lead role he has played in building the web-based systems that make the Team Development Strategy work.

I would be remiss to not thank Trent Walton, Reagan Ray, and Dave Rupert, at Paravel, for their imaginative design in helping to package and present the Team Development Strategy on the Internet. I am also grateful to John Nugent, Tom Gordon, Carolyn Greco, and Charles Kraft for their advice and for nudging me in the right directions when needed.

For their help and professional guidance in the first printing of this book, I am very grateful to Marvin D. Cloud at sopherim.com (layout and design), Russ Wright (graphics), and Joel Turner at Americas Press (printing). Their knowledge, experience, and capabilities turned a manuscript into a reality.

For the reprinting of *Team Covenant*, I sincerely thank and have great appreciation for all the talented professionals at Xlibris Corporation who have made a complex job easy, even fun at times. They include: Grace Vasquez, Publishing Consultant; Joy Daniels, Submissions Representative; Kay Benavides, Manuscript Services Representative; Vanessa Marzo, Publishing Services Supervisor; Kate Austria, Production Specialist; Michael Green, Submissions Representative; Tim Fitch, Author Services Representative; and Michael Gibson, post publications associate. Thanks to all of you, especially anyone that I inadvertently omitted. You do your jobs well!

And finally, I want to express my sincere respect and appreciation to our clients who have given us the privilege and opportunity to develop and implement the Team Covenant and the Team Development Strategy within their organizations, and to share this exciting and meaningful journey together.

INTRODUCTION

The new company had an unusual request. CompleteRx, a Houston-based hospital pharmacy management company, asked us to help develop a strategic plan for their human resources function—a rarity from an established firm, much less from a start-up. But then, CompleteRx is an unusual organization.

Led by an ambitious (some might say *foolhardy*) team of visionaries, the company's goal was to become "the employer of choice" in an industry dominated by three international giants with nearly unlimited resources. To keep from being squashed by these multinational Goliaths, CompleteRx's management knew they had to bring something more than a "me too" slingshot to the competitive arena.

So they decided to arm themselves with a bold new company culture and HR management model that would *attract, motivate, and reward* the most talented professionals from throughout their industry.

Most new companies don't think this way. Most place their initial focus on the *widget* they're going to make or the *service* they're going to deliver. The human resources function usually morphs into being, later. In the early stages, human resource management tends to focus on "Defensive HR." The HR team merely ensures that employees get paid, benefits administered, and as few laws broken as possible. But a new company wanting a *proactive* HR strategy—an organizational development plan whose long-term goal was to become the employer of choice? To some, it seemed they were putting the cart before the horse!

In fact, it was a stroke of brilliance. From Day One, management realized that *people* are the "horse" that pulls the cart. Therefore, it makes perfect sense to craft a strategy for attracting, motivating, and retaining the "horse" best suited to pulling the company cart. The motto "people are our most valuable asset," was much more than wall-plaque platitude to the leadership of CompleteRx. It was their game-changer.

We accepted management's challenge, knowing it would be critical to learn—if possible—what it would take to become the employer of choice in that industry. For one thing, what kind of company would they need to become to attract and retain a highly skilled workforce in an industry notorious for its high turnover rate? What kind of culture would they need to build? What kind of leadership and management style would work best? What kind of internal communication systems would they have to create? What would *all* this take?

To answer these (and other) questions, we launched a large psychometric assessment (psychological research) project. We collected and studied the psychological profiles of approximately six hundred randomly selected, licensed healthcare professionals in the hospital pharmacy management industry. To the best of our knowledge, such a research project has never been done for a brand-new company—before or since.

We studied hundreds of individual profiles to find both differences and similarities. We looked at composite data to spot other trends. We studied patterns of thinking, and the ways in which these professionals expressed logic, empathy, interpersonal respect, group interaction, individualism and personal independence. We also explored how trust is expressed *and* developed, where structure and attention to detail fit into individual needs and expectations, and where motivation and personal identity played a role in people's sense of achievement and lasting job satisfaction.

There were more, but this gives you a sense of what the project entailed. With the results in hand, we created an abstract of what the organization's philosophy and belief system would have to look like to create a work environment and culture that would respond to these workers' most critical needs and desires. Then, we took the abstract to our client and asked two key questions:

Could these entrepreneurs build and lead their business by applying this philosophy and belief system? Did they personally *buy into* this philosophical abstract?

Would they let us hold them accountable in their leadership performance by listening openly and objectively to constructive feedback as the process began?

The client responded with a resounding "Yes" to both questions, and with that, we began designing their strategic HR vision. Out of that study and plan was born the Team Covenant—the foundation for the type of culture, management style, and employee involvement needed to attract, motivate, and sustain/maintain the commitment of this company's professionals.

Since then, we have validated again and again that these Team Covenant principles and the Team Development Strategy are necessary ingredients for attracting and retaining the best talent in today's emerging workforce. And since then, CompleteRx has enjoyed meteoric success. By their fifth year, they had achieved more than $105 million in annual sales—a miraculous feat in their industry. That year, the company also won the Ernst & Young *Entrepreneur of the Year Award* in their category and ranked among Houston's Top 100 companies for six consecutive years. CompleteRx was on the Top 10 list for three of those years, and was ranked #1 on its fifth year.

Despite the fact that the company operates in an industry that has experienced 23 percent annual turnover nationally for more than twelve years, CompleteRx has experienced an average annual turnover rate of just 3 percent (or less) for each of the fifteen years since its founding. What's more, the company's annual employee satisfaction surveys consistently show that 80 percent to 90 percent of their employees believe CompleteRx is *the best place they have ever worked.*

Unlike their competition, the established giants that spend millions each year on recruiting new workers, CompleteRx has job applicants waiting in a long line. Several hundred unsolicited resumes are on file from highly qualified professionals—people dying to come to work for them.

It goes without saying that our client achieved its goal of becoming the industry's employer of choice—an accomplishment credited in part to the Team Covenant and Team Development Strategy. In the years which followed, the principles of the Team Covenant (TC) and the processes that comprise the Team Development Strategy (TDS) have been applied to a growing variety of organizations—for-profit, nonprofit, small, mid-sized and large—with astonishing results.

Whenever we're hired by a new client, we almost always face this same make-or-break challenge: convincing managers *and* employees that the TC and TDS *will* make a big, positive, and lasting impact on the organization's bottom line. We continually struggle to demonstrate that this program will produce results, not empty clichés and meaningless mission statements designed to look good on the organization's brochures and signage.

A thirty-one-year-old professional, working for an organization that we helped bring back from near-dead, said, "When I first heard all this TDS stuff, I thought: 'Yeah, I've heard all that before.' But this is the first place I've ever been where they really mean it and live it. This process keeps a constant scoreboard in front of me that lets me know how I'm doing and where I stand. And that's what I need and want."

This employee's before *and* after reactions are something we hear all the time. Although the Team Excellence program has received two *Impact Awards* from the Society for Human Resources Management—in Organizational Development and Employee Development—a great many employees and managers are cynical when we first introduce this revolutionary performance management system.

They have a right to be cynical.

Many employees have been exposed to performance reviews, personality tests, and employee satisfaction surveys. These elements may bear a *superficial resemblance* to the components of our program, but the similarities end there. For one thing, these individual components have never *before* been integrated into a system based on rewards and accountability. For another thing, no other program has directly tied *objective measurements* of employee strengths, competencies, and preferences to management strengths, competencies and preferences in order to create policies for improving compensation, communication, recruiting, retention, motivation, and productivity—and held employees *and* management accountable for their continued success or for not performing up to plan or meeting expectations.

Based on a written agreement between the organization and its employees (The Team Covenant), our business process integrates three proprietary systems of accountability that encompass every level of

the organization. Our system rewards performance and requires every employee to accept personal ownership for measured successful work. It also applies a values-based process to establish quantified benchmarks for doing the job—and doing it right. The Team Covenant is an integral component of our award-winning approach to measuring accountability: The Team Development Strategy. The Team Covenant and the Team Development Strategy go beyond typical mission statements or expressions of core values. They are a psychological contract for improving behavior *and* performance among every member of the organization.

At first, most employees assume that our program is just another waste of their time. After all, most have endured performance reviews before— annual reviews in which they get the "ice cream sandwich" treatment: First, the supervisor recites a list of their shortcomings; then they're given a pat on the back for some small triumphs, and finally, they're told to do a better job, even when the supervisors *don't actually know* what their jobs are and how to do them better.

What's more, the results of the performance reviews are frequently disregarded. Every employee still receives roughly the same cost of living adjustment, "merit raise" or bonus. Or, in another frequent scenario, the whole evaluation process is so riddled with office politics that some employees would rather undergo a 360° review with members of the Spanish Inquisition than their bosses and coworkers.

Meanwhile, many managers have seen one gang of HR "experts" after another come and go—all promising to reduce turnover, improve communications, increase productivity, etc.—but whose "solutions" were vague, short-term, gimmicky or too limited in scope. The solutions often required ongoing (and costly) interventions from the consultants when it came to administering tests and interpreting data and/or the expensive licensing and training (plus regular updates to software and training) of the in-house personnel who were expected to perform consultative functions.

In most cases, though, performance management programs don't succeed because management isn't really committed to them—and this applies to our Team Development Strategy as well. When faced with human resources issues ranging from shortages of qualified labor and bargain-basement morale to head-spinning turnover, it's common for senior managers to suddenly "get serious" about the problems. But what separates the successful from the unsuccessful organizations is that the

former are committed to changing their culture, communications style, and compensation policies, while the latter are merely trying to con their employees into believing "we care" by issuing memos, convening meetings and paying lip service to change. To reap the benefits of the Team Covenant and Team Development Strategy, management must be willing to walk the walk, not just talk the talk.

This program is not a quick fix. It requires dedication and a most serious commitment. Most of all it requires enormous effort and perseverance. If you aren't serious about *living* the Team Covenant and *following* the Team Development Strategy—if your aim is simply to pacify your workforce with a few platitudes and some happy talk—your situation *will* deteriorate. In fact, your organization may find itself in much worse condition after a half-hearted attempt to implement our program than if you hadn't bothered with the program at all. Employees don't like having their expectations raised and then dashed. They will get *more* than a little upset if they come to believe that management wasn't really serious about improving the work environment, or if they think management was treating them like a bunch of gullible children.

This book maps out a business process that, with ongoing senior-level commitment and participation, transforms an organization and its culture into one of metrics-driven accountability from top to bottom. The process, the tools, and the models of behavior outlined in this book can measurably improve work performance and business outcomes, substantially reducing operating costs, employee turnover, and wasted time. If you decide you want to take this journey, be prepared to finish.

# Chapter 1
WHO CARES?

A friend said to me, "I'm not sure *what* my father did for a living. He worked at IBM for twenty-five years, but whenever my sister and I asked about his job, he changed the subject. By the time I was ten, I began to suspect that 'IBM' was a cover story, and that he actually worked for the Mafia... or the CIA.

"One day, when I was about fourteen, I finally *insisted* that he reveal his job title and some specifics about his role and responsibilities. He sighed, 'I'm vice president in charge of collecting a paycheck. Who cares?'"

"*That,*" my friend said, "is typical of most people's attitude toward work. They don't really care about their jobs."

I disagree. But I *do* understand what's behind the widespread perception that most employees don't care about their jobs.

APATHY VS. FUTILITY

Once upon a time, I was invited to visit Chicago to speak. I was to be the Friday luncheon speaker at the end of a weeklong conference. I arrived in Chicago Friday morning, and reached McCormack Place early enough to sit in the audience and listen to a couple of speakers ahead of me.

I will never forget this one guy. His presentation taught me something extraordinarily important. It may be why this book ultimately was written.

The man stood in front of thousands of people, and with great passion—the passion of a pulpit-pounding preacher invoking fire and brimstone—said, "The greatest problem in America today is apathy!" The words were barely out of his mouth when some joker behind me turned to his neighbor and said, "Who cares?"

I'm not making that up. To this day, I don't know if the guy behind me was trying to be funny or had a Freudian slip. Doesn't matter. What matters is that the speaker was wrong. I took exception then, and I'm convinced to this day that apathy is not a major problem facing this country, at least not for most people.

The word "apathy" means that you don't care, and I strongly believe that most people *do* care. They care a lot. Ever since that trip to Chicago, I've been asking audiences through a show of hands if they care. Invariably, everyone raises his hand to say that he does. It's my professional judgment that you just cannot get more scientific than that.

What do you think? Do you care? Do you want to be a good person? Do you want to be a good spouse or parent? Do you want to be a good employee, manager, neighbor, and citizen?

I expect you answered "yes" to all of these questions. Most people do. Assuming that you *did* say "yes" the next question is, "Why are you so special?" No offense intended, but on this issue, you're not special. As a rule, people do care, so apathy can't be the problem. Apathy means that you don't care. But there's another term frequently confused with apathy, and that is *futility*. Futility suggests that you do care—maybe a great deal—but that no matter how hard you try, no matter how many extra miles you walk, you are powerless to affect outcomes. You are a modern-day Cassandra—a tragic figure who frets and struts upon the organization's stage, desperate to avert the next catastrophe, but whose wisdom will always be ignored by the gods of management. Hence, the results are preordained. There's nothing you can do about them. This leaves you with two options: (1) quit the job or (2) retreat into a shell of cynicism, lest your frustration be mistaken for insubordination.

The greatest problem facing organizations is not apathy. The problem is employees' sense of futility. Futility occurs when you're not kept fully informed of what's going on around you, and when you don't know where you stand. Futility occurs when you're not allowed to think or make decisions on your own; when you aren't sure what you're supposed to be doing. Futility rears it *seemingly* apathetic head when creative problem-solving by employees, who usually know what works and what doesn't, is discouraged. Futility happens when you aren't allowed to express your ideas or point of view, and you're not given a *voice* in the work you do.

High-performing managers and employees *do* care. These people want more than just a job; they want a lasting relationship based on mutual respect and trust—one backed by a sincere commitment on the part of the organization's leadership. Human relationships really matter.

When employees are told to be compliant, told *they* as individuals aren't all that important, and told their point of view and experiences are stupid, *THAT* generates futility. Futility—not apathy—is the chief obstacle to success in the business world.

If futility is the chief obstacle, *motivation* is the chief facilitator of employee satisfaction and productivity, and a powerful catalyst for *innovation.* Believe it or not, however, money is not the prime motivator for most employees. Don't get me wrong: job candidates will not bust down the door to Human Resources if you promise low wages with few or no benefits. Money does play an important role. But study after study show that financial compensation is not the most powerful employee motivator.

According to a Society of Human Resource Management (SHRM) white paper, "pay might not matter as much as you think in turnover decisions, as compensation and pay satisfaction are relatively weak predictors of employees' decisions to leave. Thus, offering pay increases or bonuses to keep people at your organization may not be the most efficient way to address retention."

This reinforces what most HR professionals have long known—that employee satisfaction and motivation are tied to various factors. The theory of *organizational equilibrium,* for example, states that employees will stay with an organization as long as the inducements, including good pay, working conditions, and developmental opportunities, are equal to (or greater than) the employee's contributions of time and effort. In other words, people stay with an organization as long as they feel they're getting as much (or more) from the company as they give.

A client once asked me to address the question of how to motivate employees at his annual meeting. While introducing me, the CEO was kind enough to pay me some compliments and build credibility for me with the audience. When I took the microphone, I thanked him for his generous remarks, and repeated the fact that I'd been asked to address the question of how to motivate employees. To everyone's dismay, I said, "You can't." I thanked them for inviting me and started walking offstage. Just as I was getting beyond view, while hearing a buzz of uncomfortable chatter throughout the hotel ballroom, I returned to the podium and said, "But if you'd like to know how you can get employees to *motivate* themselves, I have a few ideas I'd like to share."

I don't normally pull stunts like that, but it made a fundamental point: *You cannot motivate anyone else.* Motivation is an internal choice that people must make for themselves. No matter how badly you want someone to be motivated and achieve a particular outcome, they must personally want to achieve the outcome for it to occur

In his bestselling book *Drive: The Surprising Truth About What Motivates Us,* author Daniel H. Pink identifies three core elements of motivation:

Autonomy. People need to sense the value of their individuality. They want to own their achievements. They want to self-direct the pursuit of their most important goals and dreams without continual interference.

Mastery. People want to be good at what they do, and some want to be the very best. To achieve this goal, they must acquire awareness, skills, and knowledge. They must also be allowed to become the "masters and commanders" of their domains.

Purpose. People crave purpose in almost everything they do. We all want to discover greater meaning in our lives, and we all strive to make a difference. If someone sees no purpose or value in what he does, his only aspiration will be to become "vice president in charge of collecting a paycheck."

When employees are given opportunities to achieve autonomy, mastery, and purpose, they are highly motivated to become better at their jobs. When they're allowed to claim ownership for their success, they're more willing to be accountable when they are less than successful. Ultimately, the emotional rewards of work are what keep people happy and what motivates them to persevere against even daunting odds. When employees' sense of autonomy, mastery, and purpose is absent, most will succumb to futility.

What are the costs and impact of futility? It depends on the organization, but clients that have adopted our Team Development Strategy and Team Covenant have reduced their annual turnover rates from as much as 23 percent to 3 percent and maintained these results for as long as fourteen consecutive years… and counting. This represents millions of dollars (every year) in reduced operating costs, including the costs of recruitment and hiring, training, loss of performance, absenteeism, and much more.

Companies that find agreement with our Team Covenant have learned that our philosophy is simple and extremely profit-oriented. The process becomes a contract between the organization and each employee—one based on defined rules of respect for individuals and teams, coupled with clearly defined and measurable job performance expectations. All of this is negotiated in exchange for the genuine and consistent acceptance of measurable individual accountability from every manager and employee.

TODAY'S EMPLOYEES HAVE
HIGHER EXPECTATIONS

When it comes to their jobs and careers, today's employees have higher expectations than their fathers and grandfathers. Like most things, work ethic and expectations of work have evolved and continue to evolve. Various milestones in this attitudinal evolution can be benchmarked as follows:

- Traditional (the generations that fought WWI and WWII).
- Baby Boomers (the generation born between 1946 and 1964).
- Generation X (born between 1965 and 1979).
- Generation Y (born between 1980 and 1995).
- Generation Z (born after 1995).
- *Note: Today we refer to those reaching young adulthood around the year 2000 or later as Millennials.*

Younger employees expect work to be an integrated and noncompeting component in their overall lifestyles. They want a balance between time devoted to work and time devoted to family, social activities, and other responsibilities. Realistic or not, younger people expect work to be a complementary and cohesive component in their lives—not an all-consuming preoccupation I respectfully call these thirty-something and younger employees the *emerging workforce*. Businesses that hope to successfully recruit, motivate, and sustain the commitment of these employees must recognize the changes in expectations, and find new ways to address them. Consider the following:

- Workers thirty-five and younger are accustomed to instant gratification, due to the technologically driven world they have always known.

- The old employment paradigm demanded that you work your butt off for forty years and then retire to enjoy your life. As we say in Texas, "That dog won't hunt anymore."

- Younger workers have different expectations about male and female roles, (sharing home and parenting responsibilities), recreation time versus work time, the importance of making social contributions, etc.

- We live in a world of instant communication (cell phones, cable and satellite television access to the entire world as news breaks 24/7). Instant communications have fostered instant expectations. If it *can* happen now, it *should* happen now, or even *must* happen now. Postponing most of life's pleasures until you earn them is a thing of the past. This thinking dovetails with the point above about instant gratification in all aspects of our lives.

- A phrase that did not exist fifteen years ago is now part of everyone's lexicon: work/life balance. People expect more work/life balance, but many companies are only beginning to grasp the implications. Some smaller companies haven't even "gotten the memo" yet

Organizations would be well served to recognize how essential it is for people to "have fun" and enjoy their work. If people don't like what they're doing, they can't possibly do their jobs well. I'm not suggesting that work should be a fiesta (or siesta), but employees must derive satisfaction from their work. Otherwise, no amount of financial or other material incentives will effectively motivate and retain workers. Companies need to understand this belief and legitimize it—not just as "acceptable" but as essential to continuous growth.

People don't want to accept jobs or careers merely as a way to earn money for eight hours a day so they can then go home and enjoy their "real lives." Today and for the foreseeable future, work has to provide more meaning and purpose. It does this by adding value and quality to one's total lifestyle, not detracting from it. This shift in career expectations isn't new. These changes have been occurring for several generations as part of larger changes within our society.

My parents' expectations were that you took a job for life. *My* generation expected to have a number of different jobs during their careers. Today's employees expect to have multiple jobs in multiple careers during their lives. People just entering the workforce today will occupy jobs that haven't even been dreamed of yet. It's vital for companies to recognize that the new reality is already here and to understand that it's not necessarily negative. If harnessed correctly, these changes can become a powerful force for motivating increased performance and profits. They can help organizations achieve many bottom-line benefits while helping employees enjoy greater job satisfaction.

Shrewd business leaders must rethink their assumptions and behavior, and carefully assess their own values and expectations. They must determine what changes in leadership style and performance are required of them. Leaders who refuse to rethink assumptions or budge from old-school beliefs about managing solely from an autocratic power base will find it harder to attract qualified employees and, therefore, harder to successfully compete in the global marketplace.

Too many executives are not as focused on these issues as they should be. Coming out of the current recession, most of the attention has been on financial survival instead of the "soft sciences" of human behavior and HR management. At Team Excellence, we've been telling everyone that if they've tried to exploit the recent "buyer's market" and take shortcuts on commitments to existing employees, there will be a dire price to pay when the market turns around. Employees will abandon ship as quickly as possible. Many companies have debited this account more than they know.

The traditional military approach used by many management teams, which disseminates information on a "need to know" basis, no longer works. In fact, this approach will be disastrous in the future. Organizations and managers must be as proactive as possible when it comes to sharing information with employees. This means that organizations must also do a better job of *listening* to employees. Employees don't expect to get their way on every issue, but they *do* expect managers to listen, give them a voice, and acknowledge and respect their points of view, experience, and expertise.

Organizations must give people permission to be who they are instead of demanding that they be something they're not. Most employees spend too much time and energy trying to be what they *think* their bosses want them to be. Through our assessment tools, we help companies give people permission to be who they *are*, and to build tolerance (understanding and acceptance) of different work preferences and styles. This is a major factor in successful performance management. PSI is our proprietary tool for building a common, easy-to-understand, and non-judgmental language.

Although people expect to be given a voice in how work gets done, that doesn't mean employees expect to be in charge and make every decision. Instead, they want to be shown a level of individual respect for their knowledge, experience, and expertise that's often been ignored in the past. When given sincere respect, employees *want* to become part of something more than just occupying a chair. They really *want* to take ownership for results.

THE FUTURE DEMANDS MORE EMPLOYEE ENGAGEMENT

In today's world, success requires companies to become leaner and more competitive. The days of holding on to market share are gone. Companies will grow or die. This demands more flexibility, productivity, and accountability from employers and employees. Results are the only thing that matter. Blame games and perfunctory adherence to outdated and/or unproductive policies and procedures are worse than a waste of time and energy: they generate futility.

But just as organizations are beginning to recognize the need to become more streamlined and competitive, they're also facing shortages of qualified labor: "Demographic shifts (aging populations, declining birthrates, economic migration), social evolution, inadequate educational programs, globalization, and entrepreneurial practices (outsourcing, offshoring, on-demand employment) are... causing [labor] shortages, not only in the overall availability of talent but also—and more significantly— in the specific skills and competencies required," reports Manpower Inc.

More and more observers agree that a talent scarcity is looming—and that this shortage will make finding and keeping the right people with the right skills increasingly challenging for organizations. In a SHRM survey of HR professionals, 62 percent of the respondents reported already having difficulty hiring workers with the skills essential for a twenty-first-century workforce. Many business leaders worry that this problem will worsen with important demographic shifts (such as waves of retirement among aging workers). Inadequate educational systems, increasingly mobile employees, and even generational differences in perceptions about the nature of work and careers will all likely aggravate matters further. HR professionals who take time now to create strategies for dealing with these developments will put their organizations at a competitive advantage.

Meanwhile, "nearly one quarter of all U.S. workers quit their jobs in 2006, and in some industries the turnover rate is considerably higher." Although those figures may have dropped, thanks to the buyer's market of the recent recession, they will no doubt return to previous levels—and possibly skyrocket—once the market fully recovers and employees enjoy more employment options, as well as leverage, with their current employers. But even much smaller turnover rates are extremely costly.

Research suggests that direct replacement costs per employee can reach 50 percent to 60 percent of the employee's annual salary, with the total costs associated with turnover ranging from 90 percent to 200 percent of annual salary, reports W. F. Cascio in *Managing Human Resources*. This means, for example, that a high tech firm would have to spend as much as $200,000 to replace a single engineer who commanded a salary of $100,000—and that *does not* include the salary of the replacement engineer. In *Retaining Intellectual Capital in the 21st Century*, R. D. Sommer reveals that one study estimated that turnover-related costs represent more than 12 percent of pre-tax income for the average company and nearly 40 percent for companies at the 75th percentile turnover rate.

Please note that when some workers are overcome by futility, they do not quit their jobs. Instead, they become actively disengaged. I know "actively disengaged" sounds like an oxymoron, but it means that they turn off, tune out, and stop trying. Worse, disgruntled employees frequently contribute to lower morale, lower productivity, higher absenteeism, and increased tension between managers and workers. According to a 2002 Gallup poll, disengaged workers cost U.S.-based organizations more than $250 billion a year.

A 2006 *Gallup Management Journal* survey revealed that 59 percent of U.S. employees are actively disengaged. "The survey showed a strong relationship between worker happiness and workplace engagement. Happy and engaged employees are much more likely to have a positive relationship with their boss, are better equipped to handle new challenges and changes, feel they are more valued by their employers, handle stress more effectively, and are much more satisfied with their lives." Once again, relationships matter.

Unfortunately, many managers are unaware of the high costs associated with employee turnover and disengagement, dismissing these problems as "touchy-feely" intangibles. Often, management is so preoccupied with the "hard sciences" of systems and processes that they neglect the basic fact that highly trained, skilled *people* are needed to manage and operate those systems and processes. People are not interchangeable cogs in a machine, and should not be treated as such.

A few years ago, I got myself in real trouble posting the following statement on our website's homepage: "Management is maintaining the status quo. Leadership is inspiring people toward the future." The CFO of one of our clients' customers saw this, and called me on the carpet, telling me he was a Harvard-trained manager, and that he knew how to do a lot more than maintain the status quo. He was offended, and even encouraged my client to stop using our services. (They are still one of our largest clients.)

It was a semantic misunderstanding, of course, and he missed the point: I was challenging managers to get into the heads of employees to get them excited about innovation.

Experience has taught me that many managers see their jobs as keeping all the established processes and procedures running smoothly and making sure everyone gives priority to the organization's systems over critical thinking and creative problem-solving. That results in building bureaucracies, not thriving entrepreneurial businesses.

Historically, one viable business paradigm stated that companies could succeed by protecting their share of the market and maintaining the status quo. Today, that's simply no longer possible or even realistic. In the current economy, companies are doing one of two things—growing or dying. It's one or the other, and no company can survive by continuing to do what it has always done.

I was reminded of this by a new client—a nonprofit organization that's existed for more than one hundred years. This client was still using typewriters when they engaged our services, and hadn't changed many of its business processes for over thirty years. The board had just hired a new CEO, who brought in a new COO. That's when the changes began.

When we started work, we found an inefficient, unproductive, and dying organization employing ninety-five people—most of whom were afraid to think, ask questions, or do anything but keep their heads down in an effort to preserve their jobs. The organization also suffered from a severe case of what I like to call "entitlement disease." All employees expected to receive 2 percent to 4 percent annual cost of living raises because they had always received them. Performance-based compensation didn't exist.

Today, this organization is much more efficient. It has thirty-eight employees, state-of-the-art technology, and remains lean and mean by using consultants in lieu of internal staffing for certain expertise and skills. We're excited about the client because they're well on their way. A complete redevelopment of their marketing strategy and brand positioning has been accomplished, and a whole new senior leadership team was recruited and installed about two years ago.

One of the veterans recently said that she is working harder than ever before, doing new things and having the time of her life. She's enjoying a level of satisfaction she never thought possible. Although this lady is only a couple of years from retirement, I asked her about her vision. She said that she wants to leave the legacy of the new function she's been allowed to create—a function for which she feels a real sense of entrepreneurial ownership and pride. After retirement, she still wants to belong to the organization and plans to return for occasional visits to encourage and continue mentoring younger employees. The organization's leaders have inspired her toward the future.

WHAT DO YOU REALLY BELIEVE?

I would like you and your organization to benefit from our business process. I mean that. We're very proud of it, and we know it works. I know our Team Development Strategy and Team Covenant can make a substantial contribution to the growth and development of your business, as well as the lasting satisfaction of every staff member. I want that to happen for many reasons—reasons well beyond personal economic gain or advantage.

But the reality is that our process won't work for everyone. It's simply not the right strategy for every organization, and if our process is undertaken for the wrong reasons—or because the real reasons are misunderstood—it can do more harm than good.

Many organizations engage consultants or buy programmed solutions with the expectation that conducting some event will solve their problems or meet their needs. These events usually serve as "psychological suntans," especially when they're not followed up and reinforced by ongoing leadership behavior that supports and builds on the intent of the intervention.

The outcomes are usually more negative than positive because the psychological suntans fade quickly and only remind employees of the gulf between "what is" and "what should be." Sometimes, the biggest contribution from this new awareness is the acceleration of turnover. Obviously, this is a costly mistake. Senior leadership is often too busy to get involved in organizational change.

Frequently, the admonition is "go down there and solve our problems," because "my time is very limited." Employees don't respond well to a "do as I say, not what I do" environment—one where the desired changes are something employees are expected to accomplish but not the leadership.

One of the greatest barriers to achieving successful organizational change, therefore, is a lack of a sincere commitment on the part of an organization's leadership to changing their own approach.

If you're a business owner or leader, it is *essential* that you know, with clarity, what you believe, what you want, and what you are willing to do to change your organization. Even more important, you must determine just how far you're personally willing to go to modify your own thinking and behavior.

Regrettably, we've had a few clients with senior managers who did not adequately understand the importance of their roles, and did not make genuine commitments to sustained support and involvement. When the change process got too tough—and this process isn't easy—they fell back on "old school" ideas and behaviors. Their organizations and employees paid a heavy price. Often, the biggest price paid by these organizations was accelerated turnover and the associated costs, which is the opposite of what our successful clients achieve.

In the best of situations, there is still a fundamental issue that too many leaders miss. They just don't understand the process. They just don't get it! I'm talking about managers who say they want more accountability from all of their employees but mean something totally different—or don't mean it at all. To make matters worse, some leaders don't even know that they're sending contradictory messages to the staff.

I've been privileged to work with more than one hundred companies in my career, both large and small. So I know the problem isn't limited to any particular size of company, select geographies, or industry. It's pretty darn universal.

I can't honestly recall meeting a manager who did not claim to want his employees, *all of his employees*, to accept greater accountability for their work. Every leader says this. Every leader believes he really *means* it. But the reality is that some leaders don't want this.

In my experience, most managers behave more from intuition than from well-planned philosophies and strategies. What this translates into is a mind-set of *do it the way I tell you to do it.* Most managers truly don't want increased accountability. They believe that they lose control by doing that.

What they really want is "compliance," and nothing raises a bigger barrier to building a culture based on accountability than consistent daily droning messages of: *"Do it my way. I don't want you to think. I just want you to do it the way I told you!"* A culture based on compliance, whether tacit or openly acknowledged, eliminates creativity, innovation, and the self-directed ownership of successful results.

The Team Development Strategy coupled with its Team Covenant contract requires all managers and employees to accept an entrepreneurial sense of ownership for their individual roles and the accomplishment of their responsibilities. This is negotiated in return for a work environment that genuinely respects the input and value of individuals. It's part of the deal.

The process requires the investment of time and consistent, never-ending demonstrations of interest, support, and encouragement from the organization's leadership—leadership that believes in rewarding performance and accountability, not just compliance. Accountability must become the standard of performance for a Team Covenant organization.

This standard rewards successful achievement and performance. It is diametrically opposed to the traditional organizational culture based on entitlement. Questions we must all answer:

- Whether you're a leader or an employee, what do you believe?
- What are you willing to commit to accomplishing these aims?
- What kind of a culture do you want?
- Do you want to be rewarded for what you do, or merely for showing up?
- Are you afraid of accountability, or are you ready to embrace it?

THE TEAM COVENANT IN ACTION: A CASE HISTORY

Colin Hathaway was prepared to commit his company to becoming a Team Covenant organization. The president and CEO of Seattle-based AZ-Tech Inc. had designed a corporate culture that reflected his mission to improve employees' quality of life and safeguard the environment while also driving economic growth for both the company and the local community.

To date, the mission had been an unqualified success. Having joined AZ-Tech straight out of college—at a time when the company had fewer than 100 employees—Colin now leads a corporation with six branches, 4,600 employees, and $1.3 billion in annual revenues. Growth was projected at 9.4 percent for the next 12 months, and 22 percent for the next five years. He'd had his cake and eaten it, too.

But today, it has become increasingly obvious that Colin's business practices were about to collide with some inconvenient truths. Over the last five years, much of AZ-Tech's growth had come through acquisitions. That meant assimilating hundreds of new employees from a variety of diverse employment backgrounds. Lately, the once homogenous corporate culture had been transformed into a high-tech "Tower of Babel." More and more, communication was breaking down as the "nuclear family" grew into a confederation of warring "tribes."

Several key product rollouts had been delayed, while the software engineers argued over last-minute upgrades and enhancements, driving his senior vice president of marketing, Kelly Anderson, to the brink of madness. Even worse, one of their newest products debuted to a market that had almost no interest in the software—a classic case of designing a product that customers may have needed, but didn't want.

Colin understood that the technology industry is composed of brilliant and creative people—programmers, designers, and "imaginers"—who benefit from unstructured work environments and more democratic styles of management, but things were getting out of control. Every high-tech firm needs to stay ahead of the innovation curve, but it also needs to SELL things in the meantime. AZ-Tech needed to strike the right balance between managed business processes and chaotic creative freedom. It needed to reinvent its corporate culture to deal with a necessarily larger and more diverse workforce and corporate structure.

When Kelly Anderson's assistant (whom she'd brought with her seven years earlier from the Fortune 100 where they'd both worked) introduced her to Team Excellence, Kelly leapt at the opportunity. After a presentation and a follow-up conference call, Team Excellence was retained to design and implement a new, customized performance management system for the company.

Colin hoped the Team Covenant and Team Development Strategy would help recreate the culture and business practices that had fueled the company's remarkable growth and profitability (but on a larger scale), using a structured, metrics-driven system. In fact, he was literally banking on it.

NOTE: Though this case history is technically "hypothetical," it mirrors the actual people, circumstances, problems, and experiences of several Team Excellence clients. We believe this "composite case history," which we'll revisit again and again throughout the book, will provide a detailed, "ground-level" view of how the Team Covenant and Team Development Strategy works in the real world.

Chapter 2
THIS ISN'T "TOUCHY-FEELY"

In the movie *Office Space*, software engineer Peter Gibbons is so overwhelmed with futility (and accidentally hypnotized into a state of perpetual ennui) that he stops going to work. He doesn't see any point to it. When he decides to swing by the office to collect a few personal things, however, he discovers that his boss has hired efficiency experts Bob Porter and Bob Slydell to "trim the fat." With nothing to lose, Peter tells the two consultants how he *really* feels about his job:

BOB SLYDELL

Y'see, what we're trying to do here, we're just trying to get a feel for how people spend their day. So, if you would, would you just walk us through a typical day for you?

PETER

Well, I generally come in at least fifteen minutes late. I use the side door, that way Lumbergh [the boss] can't see me. Uh, and after that, I just sorta space out for about an hour.

BOB PORTER

Space out?

PETER

Yeah I just stare at my desk but it looks like I'm working. I do that for probably another hour after lunch too. I'd probably, say, in a given week, I do about fifteen minutes of real, actual work.

BOB SLYDELL

Uh, Peter, would you be a good sport and indulge us and tell us a little more?

PETER

The thing is, Bob, it's not that I'm lazy. It's just that I just don't care.

BOB PORTER

Don't, don't care?

PETER

It's a problem of motivation, all right? Now, if I work my ass off and Initech ships a few extra units, I don't see another dime. So where's the motivation? And here's another thing, Bob. I have eight different bosses right now!

BOB SLYDELL

I beg your pardon?

PETER

Eight bosses.

BOB SLYDELL

Eight?

PETER

Eight, Bob. So that means when I make a mistake, I have eight different people coming by to tell me about it. That's my real motivation—not to be hassled. That and the fear of losing my job, but y'know, Bob, it will only make someone work hard enough not to get fired.

The consultants decide that this young go-getter has "straight-to-upper management written all over him." The problem lies with Peter's boss, who hasn't sufficiently motivated him.

THE PROBLEMS WITH CONVENTIONAL PERFORMANCE MANAGEMENT

Other than the fact that *Office Space* has become a cult classic that (unfortunately) resonates with many office workers, I introduced this scene because:

1. The brutally frank assessment offered by Peter, along with the consultants' recommendations, is *exactly* what many managers hope to glean from conventional performance reviews and psychometric testing, but rarely do.

2. Management almost never receives this kind of insight because the tools and programs offered by most consultants are limited in scope, vague in their objectives, randomly applied, and frequently hijacked for political purposes—to the point where no sane employee would *dare* speak truth to anyone in power.

3. Many leaders regard performance management as an expensive waste of time.

The behavioral sciences are often referred to as "soft sciences," especially in regard to management disciplines, while finance, accounting, manufacturing, engineering, information technology, etc. are considered "hard sciences." Because psychology, sociology, and other studies of human behavior and interaction are not as precise or black and white as their hard science counterparts, they haven't been considered necessary or important to how one *actually runs* an organization. My perspective has always been: *Nothing is more critical to the success of any business than the thinking and behavior of human beings.*

Another influence on perceptions of the behavioral sciences is that they haven't been regarded as *tough* and *masculine*—unlike engineering, manufacturing, etc. Consequently, since most business decisions in the past were made by men, using human psychology as part of management decision making was almost seen as illegitimate. A lot of men were uncomfortable when it came to addressing interpersonal relationships and human behavior. Though this stereotypical thinking is changing, it still has a long way to go. I hope our work will contribute to the continuing evolution in thought.

If one goal of management and leadership is to solve problems, consider the following. Which is more challenging, (1) opening a technical manual to determine how many degrees to adjust a cutter blade so one can obtain the precise dimension needed on a coil of flat-rolled steel processed through a slitter machine or (2) making an informed decision on how to coach an autocratic supervisor to communicate clearly with employees to improve performance and reduce operating expenses by 10 percent?

I rest my case.

One contribution we want to make is cleaning up some of the *sloppy* jargon surrounding performance management. I'm referring specifically to the term "touchy-feely," a phrase commonly used to describe any intervention that addresses human behavior.

To the best of my knowledge, "touchy-feely" became part of our lexicon in the 1960s and 1970s, as the self-improvement movement gained prominence and was used to describe those bare-your-soul exercises that went *way* too far in what were called T-groups and/or sensitivity training. Often, these programs were conducted by self-appointed *psycho-babble-ologists* to get the most dysfunctional members of a culture to improve their self-knowledge and self-esteem. Thankfully, the trend ground to a halt almost as fast as it started.

Although the T-group fad has mostly disappeared, "touchy-feely"— unlike "flower child," "groovy," and "right on!"—has not. In the business world, the term "touchy-feely" refers to any activity that tries to improve human behavior. If you Google the phrase, you'll find that "touchy-feely" is often used "disparagingly in contexts where hard and businesslike behavior is the norm." When I hear executives say "touchy-feely," they are usually dismissing what I do. They are saying, "This isn't important. It's just something we have to do."

Many companies publish some type of formal "touchy-feely" mission statement, purpose statement, or expression of core values. Because so many executives "talk the walk, without walking the walk," however, these statements lack credibility. Our Team Covenant takes a different approach. It is a negotiated contract, a condition of employment, between the organization and its employees. It's not a legal contract, but a psychological agreement.

If you're having trouble getting the word "covenant" to roll off your tongue, you're not alone. We chose that word carefully, to set apart what we do from the norm. The Team Covenant is a specific set of performance agreements that holds both the individual employee *and* the organization accountable. A comprehensive, metrics-driven, integrated system of performance definition and measurement, the Team Development Strategy ain't no "touchy-feely" approach. It is designed to overcome the *real* problems associated with most performance management programs:

- Too vague, nonspecific, and limited in scope.
- Considered only for performance or job appraisal. Annual performance reviews and occasional psychometric testing rarely improve motivation or performance. In fact, they are dreaded like the plague!
- Used to justify compensation decisions that were made earlier.
- When results don't please management, they are tossed in the trash.
- Too political. Some employees are afraid to speak truth to power; some managers evaluate subordinates on how well they "toe the line."
- Too expensive. Many consultants charge an arm and a leg to administer tests, interpret results, dispense licenses, certifications, etc.

Historically, performance management programs *de-motivate* employees more often than they motivate. They are usually postponed and procrastinated over because they get in the way of work. Here's how that worked out for one old-line manufacturing firm before they contacted us:

This organization didn't have a succession plan—i.e., it had no "bench." Every member of the management team was at least fifty years old, and one day, it dawned on them that nobody would be around to run the company in ten years. For the first time, the company mounted a highly focused and very expensive recruiting effort to obtain a second string of best-of-the-best MBAs, engineers, managers and executives. They hired eighteen young superstars at a total investment of $2 million-plus. The recruits were promised great career and leadership opportunities. They were also promised a state-of-the-art executive development program, which would include continuous feedback and coaching.

The recruits constantly asked for the feedback, but got none. They were told, "We'll get to it soon, but today we have a business to run." Within a year, twelve of the eighteen recruits had quit. Exit interviews pointed to a lack of feedback as the #1 reason for their hasty departures.

WHAT'S NEEDED TO MAKE PERFORMANCE MANAGEMENT WORK

To make businesses become more profitable and competitive, performance management programs need to help leadership:

1. Reduce the cost of achieving successful performance.

2. Do a better job of defining required results.

3. Adjust to new employee expectations and career/life goals.

4. Engage, motivate and gain commitment from teams of people.

5. Provide equal opportunity *without* identical treatment.

6. Become continuous coaching institutions.

7. Dedicate time and resources to make all of this happen.

Reduced Costs: I'm not talking about the direct costs of administering performance management programs, but the costs of *not* doing it. These costs include the financial drains caused by low performance; poor communications, and poorly defined expectations; mistaken assumptions (thinking that the boss sent you to Miami when he actually wanted you to go to LA); turnover, recruitment, and replacement; training and learning-curve development; and so forth.

Define Required Results: Performance management programs must do a better job of helping companies define the results they expect from both employees *and* managers. I've asked managers and workers the following question for thirty years:

ME

What do you expect John to do?

MANAGER

Oh, he knows.

ME

Everyone always says, "He knows." Please humor me, because I'm ignorant. I don't know anything about John's job or what you expect of him. Cite one, two, or three metrics that let you determine whether John has done a good job or a bad job. Write those things down.

Then I pay a visit to John.

ME

At the end of the day, how will your manager know whether you've done a good job or a bad job? What's he going to look for? What's he going to measure?

Over the decades, I've compared these two sets of lists time and time again. Guess what I've found? They never match. They NEVER match. Managers assume that employees know what to do and, as a consequence, employees' job definitions, everyday tasks, and the results they're expected to deliver are not clearly defined. *That* is one reason why many organizations waste so much time and money.

Another reason that organizations waste time and money is because most consultants in my profession are in the "project business." They sell limited-time, limited scope, "do-not-sell-past-this-date" projects offering limited deliverables. They start the project, they do the work, and then it's done. Later, they may follow up to sell you something else, or they'll go off to prospect for new clients.

The Team Development Strategy is *not* a limited-time offer. It is not (and does not necessarily need to be) administered by an elite unit of HR commandos who will swoop into your offices to implement performance evaluations and interpret the results of hundreds of Myers-Briggs Personality Type Indicators, and then flee the scene without a trace.

When we engage clients, the first question that usually comes up is, "How long will this take?" Our standard response is "Three to five years." That's how long it takes to fully redesign and begin to measure the lasting results of a new culture. Of course, there *are* immediate and positive results which can be measured from the very beginning, but lasting and permanent change takes time. In fact, the process is never-ending, though our direct involvement *does* wind down.

Our system does not allow shortcuts. As an example, for most new clients, the preferred and intuitive first step is usually the performance review component—our Performance Assessment and Review System (PARS). Most organizations know they need to do this and want to immediately improve on their current approach by launching a series of performance reviews. This is *not* an implementation strategy that will produce the best, fastest, and most lasting results. Therefore, we don't allow it.

In addition, we do not charge incrementally for any of our value-added services—a significant innovation within our industry. Our fees are packaged into retainer agreements in an "eat all you want" approach I consistently get advised that we need to offer the TDS components individually to get more business, but experience tells me that this would *not* foster the long-standing relationships we enjoy or the long-term success our clients achieve. Further, I strongly believe that our uniqueness (and the reason our system gets the results that it gets) are the products of this synergy. Therefore, we bundle the whole process.

For our competitors who offer client account management functions online, fees for the services are usually built into much higher unit pricing of $100 to $250 per instrument. (We *do* sell PSI online to individuals at www.teamexcellence.com.) Our competitors make their "real money," however, from their certification processes which provide authorization or licenses to use their instruments. These fees range from $2,000 to $5,000 for initial certification. Then they impose annual renewals or re-certifications for as much as $2,000 every year or two. One major player in this industry makes more revenue off their consultant certification and retraining fees than from sales of their survey instruments.

Adjust to New Employee Expectations and Goals: We've already covered this in depth. Remember, younger employees (particularly those thirty-five or younger), are entering careers with the expectation that there will be more balance between their personal and work lives, and they also expect more immediate satisfaction. And this evolution is no longer limited to younger workers. Many of their older colleagues are adopting this new paradigm as well. Performance management must help companies address these new career expectations and objectives.

Engage, Motivate, and Gain Commitment from Teams: We need to find new ways to engage, motivate, and gain the commitment of not just individuals but teams of individuals. That's the only way that organizations can function in today's global marketplaces. These adjustments can't be done through executive intuition alone.

Provide Equal Opportunity without Identical Treatment: I have a client—a company owned and operated by a very successful African-American. Half of his management organization is African-American. I got up in front of these guys and said, "Equal opportunity has caused this country more harm than good."

I was ready for rocks to be launched at me, however, I added, "The goal of making everybody's opportunity equal, of leveling the playing field, and giving everyone a fair chance is a morally correct direction and goal. I endorse it. It's good. We need to do that. But we've messed things up by confusing equal opportunity with identical treatment."

If I'm going to create equal opportunity within my organization, the presumption is that I have to treat everybody exactly the same. And it doesn't work for the plain and simple reason that we are *not* the same. We're all different. If you treat everybody the same, you'll be very lucky to get good performance. You'll be lucky if you properly train, coach, and mentor 15 percent to 20 percent of your workforce.

Managers tend to take the course of least resistance and treat everyone pretty much the same. Everyone receives the same amount of information, instruction, and guidance in the same formats. Everyone is exposed to the manager's same interpersonal approach (her preferred style) to instruction and instructions. Everyone has the same amount of authority and discretion to think and make decisions—or to *not* think and make *no* decisions. It's assumed that everyone possesses the same motivators and job-related interests.

Using our Personal Strengths Inventory (PSI), managers learn neutral, nonjudgmental language to understand every employee's approach to work—based on how he thinks and perceives life and work, and how he's motivated to actually perform work. The PSI language is simple, easy to learn, and gives managers the ability to know why each employee intuitively approaches work in the way he does—not the way the manager thinks he should approach the work. This tool lets managers coach and manage employees based on their individuality, not on the manager's assumptions of what is "normal." This is what I mean by equal but *not* identical treatment.

Does this also apply to hiring policies and practices?

Of course, policies and practices must be uniformed. That's the "equal" part. But applying those policies and practices with an understanding of each person's unique personality, style, motivations, etc.—through a fair but not a cookie-cutter process—is where the non-identical part comes in.

Become Continuous Coaching Institutions: This is a big point. Organizations need to become continuous coaching organizations—just as the best athletes receive continuous coaching on a daily (or near-daily) basis. In most organizations today, employees are lucky to receive *any* coaching—much less the benefits of routine and systemized coaching and mentoring. Using our process, coaching and mentoring are woven together and integrated.

It's a very simple premise. Coaching and mentoring are contemporary terms to define the most important job any manager has—*getting work done through others*. Historically, managers have done a very poor job of this. Too often, people were promoted to management because they were the best workers. (We didn't do a good job of evaluating their management skills—just their demonstrated "worker" skills.) The assumption was that if you could do your job well, you could get others to do their jobs well, and that's not necessarily true. Since most people like to keep doing the very things at which they've been most successful, many managers became "superdoers" instead of effective managers. Many don't even know the difference between "doing" and "managing," and THAT is a major source of the *reliance on compliance* instead of on *accountability*.

I sometimes use coaching and mentoring interchangeably, but I want to draw a distinction. A *coach* is someone who knows how to instruct and develop the knowledge, skills, and abilities of another to get that person to improve and do the job better. A *mentor* typically does that too, but she rises to a higher level by taking a more personal interest in the mentee, assuming an interest in his overall well-being, looking at his long-term potential, and taking responsibility for helping this person grow and develop. Mentoring is a more personal investment in the relationship.

As for coaching in general, it must be a continuous process, not an occasional event. Coaching requires consistency and follow-through. Tiger Woods may be the best golfer in the world (or was), but to remain the best, he doesn't get a monthly or even a weekly coaching lesson. He gets a daily coaching session. *That's* what is required of coaching—constant, ongoing, and persistent attention.

Dedicate Time and Resources to Make All of This Happen: Put plainly and simply, leaders must dedicate serious time and resources to pulling this off. Managing human capital is very complex, which shouldn't come as a big shock. When you're dealing with human beings, very few things are simple, and like any tool, the Team Covenant and Team Development Strategy can be used incorrectly. Remember what I said earlier about psychological suntans? If an organization undertakes our approach without a sincere commitment from top executives and instead adopts a "go down there and solve my problems" attitude, our approach will disappoint miserably. Our approach can only work with a sincere and sustained commitment—and personal involvement—from the very top of the organization.

Even worse than psychological suntans are what happens when a company deliberately intends (from the beginning) to use our approach to assess and control its staff from an old school, autocratic frame of mind. To date, we haven't had that experience, but we're convinced that some prospects wanted to do this. I'm usually personally involved in every client relationship, so I've screened out these prospects from the get go.

For instance, we recently had an inquiry from an Australian-based company that found us on the Internet. The contact came from the COO, the organization's #2 guy. For over a month, we spent loads of time on Skype laying out a strategy. After that month, the COO came back and started asking questions, telling me he was getting "some resistance" from within the organization. My research told me that their one-hundred-plus employees were mainly young professionals, and that the only "north-of-fifty" member of the organization was the CEO. I asked if the resistance was from the CEO and was told "yes." I then described in detail "old school" paradigms and leadership behavior, and the COO was literally taken aback. He was astounded that I knew what was going on.

Bottom line, we do not have *that* company as a client, and short of divine intervention, we probably won't. Companies need a performance management system that holds both managers and employees accountable for measurable results. You do not become the employer of choice in your industry by continuing to insist on "business as usual," especially when that insistence comes from the top.

Fortunately, I've been able to "influence" most organizations into taking a full bite of the program from the very get go. This isn't always the case with large organizations that have existing systems and the financial/political investments in place. Hence, some large companies start by taking advantage of the program's "psychometric magic," and take incremental "bites" from there. PSI is the correct initial step, because it develops the relational trust needed to allow the remaining performance management components to succeed.

AZ-TECH MEETS THE TDS

The day after Colin and HR Director Cheryl Bergen met with Team Excellence, the CEO called a meeting of the senior managers to acquaint them with the Team Covenant and Team Development Strategy and solicit off-the-cuff feedback. The management team included Vice President of Marketing Kelly Anderson, Senior Vice President of Operations Frank Girardi, and Vice President of Product Development Gary Monroe.

Colin knew that both Cheryl and Kelly were already on board, since he'd been in discussions with Cheryl for several months on the need to better manage and monitor employee performance, while Kelly had actually introduced him to Team Excellence.

He also expected quick *buy-in* from Gary. Though Gary knew little about managing people, he was not a fan of the autocratic "old school." The Team Development Strategy and its covenant of accountability, as well as its scoreboards and feedback, would make perfect sense to him. He represented the "emerging workforce," and his department of young overachievers would make the perfect proving ground.

On the other hand, Colin expected a little pushback from Frank—if not a bulldozing. Though only forty-one-years-old, Frank behaved like a man born twenty years earlier. Technologically shrewd and very knowledgeable about the industry, he genuinely wanted to support the CEO but lacked people skills and a thirty-thousand-foot view of the organization's mission. His management style was definitely "old school," and under stress, he was prone to emotional explosions.

He got over these "bad hair days" pretty quickly but didn't know how to express regret and didn't recognize his effect on employees. Put bluntly, he was hardly the model of a modern enlightened manager.

After taking ten minutes to summarize the challenges confronting AZ-Tech, Colin asked Cheryl to distribute copies of the Team Excellence PowerPoint Presentation, as well as our Team Covenant and the TDS *Implementation Outline*. He explained that the company was undertaking a new performance management system based on the contract before them, and that Cheryl would soon arrange orientations for all of them. Until then, he asked everyone to read over the materials and give him their impressions.

Colin wasn't so much interested in debating the merits of the new system. He'd already made up his mind to commit to the TDS. He did, however, want to gauge each executive's reactions as a way of determining the level of buy-in versus resistance he should expect from his senior staff and achieve as much genuine *individual ownership* as possible. After all, that is a fundamental (and paramount) Team Covenant requirement.

"That's all for now," he said. Everyone rose to leave, except for Frank. His face instead widened into a broad grin as he said, "Just one tiny question."

"Yes?" asked Colin.

"Shouldn't we have been waiting at the foot of Mount Sinai for a month while you had these commandments chiseled onto stone tablets?"

"I'll have Kinko's chisel some copies into granite for you, Frank."

Frank laughed and joined the others as they left the office.

Colin kept a smile frozen on his face until everyone had departed. Then he exhaled audibly before sinking into the chair behind his Lucite desk.

I had warned him that many managers enter into the process with some skepticism. Frank might be a problem, all right. How much of a problem was impossible to know. What I *did* know was that Frank took his role and responsibilities very seriously. Making wisecracks wasn't in his nature—not during office hours. Would he be ready to adapt to a fairly radical change in leadership behavior, and maybe a significant redefinition of the company's philosophy? Was he prepared to completely rethink and rearticulate his leadership and management philosophy? And what about the others? They'd smiled and said nothing, but that wasn't necessarily a good thing.

Chapter 3
THE TEAM COVENANT SOLUTION

If people are to accept personal accountability for their work, they must have a genuine sense of personal ownership of performance *and* results. To develop and sustain this sense of ownership, organizations need to promote a suitable work culture. Success requires ongoing effort. It cannot and *will not* happen overnight. Although our clients begin to measure success in the first year, it takes as long as three years for the Team Development Strategy to gain a foothold in their cultures. That's because one key ingredient in the process is total transformation of the organization's reward system.

Stop and think for a moment about the difficulties of rewarding employee performance. What has your experience been? Who gets what and why?

In most organizations, even if rewarding for performance is professed, annual increases in compensation are often based on the arbitrary distribution of allocated financial formulas. Employees get their percentage share of the total allocation, frequently influenced by the subjective decision making of supervisors and managers. These decisions are sometimes based on who the supervisors like and dislike.

Everyone will probably receive a minimum increase, usually justified as a "cost of living" consideration. Year after year, this fosters a culture of entitlement which is difficult (but not impossible) to dismantle.

Think of it this way: How can you expect employees to perform to levels of excellence if they are rewarded for being mediocre?

Businesses that reward entitlement expectations find themselves at a strong competitive disadvantage today—a disadvantage that will only increase over time. Organizations that learn how to reward performance based on *measured* contributions and achievements attract the *best of the best*, especially among the *emerging workforce*.

The Team Covenant and the Team Development Strategy establish standards of accountability, clearly negotiated definitions of performance expectations, and cross-referenced performance evaluation systems that are fair, objective, and well documented. The process offers the incentive opportunities and the measurement yardsticks needed to create a culture based on entrepreneurial ownership and accountability for individual performance. It also provides the individualized data that organizations must have to coach and mentor continuous improvement.

Managers who don't define the organization's purpose and values, and don't inform employees about them, can't expect workers to make a sincere and lasting commitment to the organization and their jobs.

Remember, *everyone* needs a sense of purpose and mission, and a clear understanding of how his contribution affects the purpose and mission of the organization. One of the most critical pieces of information that a manager can give to any employee is WHY—not just what, how, where, and when. Even assembly line workers performing the most routine tasks need to know (and want to know) *why* it's critical to bolt this component to that component in order to understand the value of their work, and spot mistakes and potential problems when they occur.

If someone has no clear—*and contextual*—understanding of her job's value and purpose, she will eventually join the legions of workers who have become "futile," whose sole motivation is to avoid being hassled or fired—like Peter Gibbons in *Office Space*. Or like my friend's father, she will "look busy" when the supervisor walks past, react to instructions without ever taking proactive measures, and spend most of her time daydreaming about her "real life" outside the office or factory.

How can employees commit to something that isn't defined or understood? Many employees often lack a mission, purpose, and sense of ownership and typically "commit" to an attitude of "us vs. them"—a very divisive and destructive mentality. And when *managers* convey this "us vs.

them" belief system, battle lines are drawn, and employee engagement, accountability, and ownership *never* happen.

The Team Covenant is a tool that addresses all of the complex factors and dynamics we've discussed so far. As a contract (albeit a psychological, not a legal contract), it establishes agreement and appropriate levels of commitment from every individual *and* the organization itself.

The word "covenant" causes pause for some, as it did for Frank. We acknowledge that. "Covenant" means mutual promise and lasting commitment, and suggests a deep and abiding agreement that should not be broken. We chose "Team Covenant" because we believe those words express more meaning and power than "Team Agreement," "Team Deal" or "Team Contract."

The Team Covenant is a contract for change between the organization and all of its managers and employees, including (and I repeat) *including* its senior-level executives. *Especially* senior-level executives. Like any good agreement, it stipulates what the contractual exchange will be. In this case, the organization promises to provide managers and employees with certain things, and in return, the organization expects certain things from every individual manager and employee.

The Team Covenant is much more specific than most mission statements, statements of core values, or clichés about the importance/value of human resources. This contract makes a very specific statement about the organization's business philosophy, commitment to customer service (internal *and* external), and the standards for both individual and team performance. It's expected that every manager and employee will accept personal accountability for their individual role in helping the organization to succeed.

Our clients use the Team Covenant as a condition of employment, and some clients ask that every manager and employee sign a copy as a symbolic demonstration of their commitment. Others ask employees to acknowledge their acceptance of the Covenant when they log into one of the online assessment systems that comprise the TDS

The chairman of the board of one statewide banking client delivers his organization's commitment to the Team Covenant through a DVD used in ongoing training and new employee orientation. The Covenant is prominently displayed by all of our clients in a variety of ways—e.g., framed documents in their boardrooms and other locations, laminated placards placed on every employee's desk, Internet and Intranet sites, etc. One client has given all employees a customized mouse pad to remind them of the organization's obligations and their individual obligations. When introduced and applied correctly, the Team Covenant serves as a *living document* that reflects the commitments of the company and its workforce to creating a special, *employer of choice*, culture. Here's a copy of the Team Covenant. To view the complete text, please turn to page 145.

1 WE AGREE to treat all employees with courtesy and respect, and to recognize the value of their individuality. We will strive to always give recognition when employees do their job well. When a job is not done well, we want to focus on "what" went wrong and "how" to correct it in the future, and not lose sight of the individual employee's worth and value. This is how we demonstrate individual dignity and respect. In return, **WE EXPECT** that each employee will always try to do their very best, assume accountability for the work they perform, and continuously attempt to grow and improve in their job.

2 WE AGREE to give all employees the right and the opportunity to express their individual points of view, to be heard, and to share in an open and honest dialogue about how we work together, without recrimination or fear of political consequences from within our organization. In return, **WE EXPECT** that each employee will always be honest, maintain total integrity, and express themselves in a courteous, mature and professional manner with everyone at all times.

3 WE AGREE to the best of our ability and within the limits of our resources to reward each employee commensurate with their demonstrated motivation and performance, and provide incentives for doing a job well. In return, **WE EXPECT** that each employee will constantly attempt to do their very best, show a desire for innovative growth and personal improvement, and strive to be excellent in all that they do.

4 WE AGREE to share information throughout our organization whenever possible, and to keep every employee as well informed as we can. We understand the need, value and importance of open communication, and we know that people perform at their best when they fully understand what is going on. In return, **WE EXPECT** each employee to communicate clearly, specifically, politely and professionally with our company's management and fellow employees as we all work together.

5 WE AGREE to take the time necessary to accomplish this overall covenant. We live and work in a highly demanding world of work, and acknowledge that time is a very difficult resource to manage. Training, organizational growth and development, and team building require time. In return, **WE EXPECT** each employee to assume the responsibility and be accountable for using time effectively, and to apply themselves fully in their participation in the implementation of this overall covenant.

6 We genuinely believe in the "Golden Rule" as meaning, treat others as you would like to be treated. This age-old guiding principle complements our organizational philosophy. **WE AGREE** to honor this rule with each employee and in return, **WE EXPECT** each employee to demonstrate this rule toward others in the performance of their job.

This team covenant should guide our daily performance and behavior. If we accomplish this, we will continue to grow as an excellent and stable company that provides secure and long-term career opportunity to each and every employee. Because we are people, we will make mistakes and may, unfortunately, sometimes fall short of our own self-determined expectations. If and when we do fall short of these expectations, we should acknowledge our mistakes, apologize for them, and sincerely promise to try harder and do better.

We are a service-driven organization with a strong sense of community. Therefore, this covenant among ourselves should extend first to each of our families, and then to our customers, suppliers, and all of the other professional relationships in which we engage. This will make us a very unique, strong and effective team.

Once again, we want each employee to experience a pride of ownership in our business and our company's success. We believe that each member of our team must find satisfaction and enjoyment in the work they do for our company, if they are to maximize their job performance and personal career experience. This team covenant is an expression of our genuine commitment to this very important and essential goal, and to the organizational culture we aspire to create and maintain.

As a team, let's move forward with excitement, optimism and enthusiasm into the successful future we can all share together.

_____   _____
        Name   **Signature**

Copyright © Team Excellence, Inc.

WHY THE TDS IS DIFFERENT

Some companies do *some* of what we do—offering a few pieces of the overall process—but none of them has assembled these components into an integrated process that's anywhere as unique and successful as ours. Most companies conduct performance appraisals, usually on an annual basis—often still a paper-and-pencil approach. Many companies use psychological testing for pre-employment screening and training or coaching. And some companies occasionally survey their employees to assess their level of satisfaction with the organization.

I could never understand why these three sets of data were always separate interventions and never considered together. Together, they represent a very comprehensive and holistic assessment of an individual and the organization. Combined, they produce a wealth of information that has significant potential to improve performance—something that's virtually impossible when you consider the data separately.

Performance appraisal information determines *what* a person is doing. Personality data tells you *why* a person does things the way he does. If you combine this data in a way that uses comparable, synergistic learning models and language, *now* you have a powerful and reliable tool to increase performance and professional growth.

If you then add relevant job and organizational satisfaction data (again using comparable learning models and language), you obtain information that's never been made available in the past. Organizations can use this information to improve the aggregate performance of managers and employees and achieve market advantages—ranging from attracting and sustaining the commitment of the best employees to improving management of operational costs. The Team Development Strategy achieves all of these goals—and more.

We've developed and integrated three proprietary software assessment tools that utilize comparable language and learning models, all in a synergistic fashion. They assess performance, personality, and behavior, as well as employee satisfaction with the job and the organization. All three systems are Web-based, providing fast, efficient, and intuitive online administration. Clients tell us they are the easiest, most user-friendly processes they've ever used. Employees find the integrated and complementary formats simple to understand and easy to apply. This business process, through client achievements, has won two important awards for its contributions to organizational and employee development from the Society of Human Resource Management (SHRM), which were awarded through its prestigious Impact Award Program.

The Team Development Strategy is a practical, seamless, metrics-driven system that allows organizations to implement the Covenant.

The total system puts in place an objective process for evaluating and measuring all the obligations of accountability that the Covenant requires, which includes holding employees accountable for *what* they accomplish, having employees hold themselves and one another accountable for *how* they communicate and work together, and (something normally missing in most organizations) having employees hold the organization accountable for fulfilling its obligations under the Covenant.

The remainder of this book explains the integrated components of the Team Development Strategy and their application. It provides an understanding of what the tools are designed to do, and how to best use them. We will map out a step-by-step approach for using the TDS, and share the sequence and timing that's worked best for most organizations. If the Team Covenant philosophy is in keeping with what you believe, and if you're willing to make the commitment, you can use this process to facilitate entrepreneurial ownership and accountability that will fuel prosperity and growth.

THIS KOOL-AID ISN'T FOR EVERYONE

I started my career as the training manager for a division of one of the largest conglomerates in the world. This group of companies had its hand in nearly every pie you can imagine—from shipbuilding and natural gas to picking lettuce. As I became familiar with my counterparts and their divisional management staffs, what struck me most was pervasive "old school" thinking. This way of thinking holds that the only way to get work done through others (the textbook definition of management) is through the use of power and control.

Old-school managers believe that you cannot expect employees to accept responsibility or accountability for their work. And yet, these managers are the first to voice a loud "You bet!" when asked if they want employees to accept greater personal accountability. Old-school managers lack the most critical component needed to build a successful Covenant relationship, and that component is *trust*.

Without trust, there cannot be a relationship of mutual respect—of self-directed and self-assumed ownership for results. When managers don't trust their employees, employees are not about to accept accountability for anything.

I've learned the important lesson that trust must always be a two-way street. Anything short of that is artful pretending and sometimes not very artful. More important, I've also learned that the amount of trust that an individual gives to another individual is a reliable measure of the trust they're worthy of receiving.

Let's cut to the chase and take a quick barometer reading. Where are you philosophically on all of this? What do you believe about people, trust, power, and control? Are you an old-school thinker or are you really open to other ideas?

Please be honest with yourself. I've seen many managers profess openness to something other than old-school thinking, until the guacamole hits the fan over a critical financial issue. What sounded fashionable suddenly makes no sense and creates conflicts in terms of priorities—and maybe their sense of self-preservation.

Here's what we do *not* want to happen. Organizations do themselves significant harm when they profess one philosophy and follow another. I say this from too much experience. When senior-level executives create expectations on the part of their employees—by installing a business process based on self-directed performance, open communications, mutual and respectful trust, and shared responsibilities and accountabilities—and THEN manage their organizations using old-school "my way is best" behavior, performance goes down, and stress, turnover, operating costs go up. The enterprise suffers and is worse off than if nothing had been done at all.

When they reflect genuine commitment AND sustained participation from an organization's senior leadership, the Covenant and Team Development Strategy help build a culture of self-motivated employees willing to own their piece of the business, and also willing to be held accountable for results. Over and over again, we see them becoming *intrepreneurs*—employees who think and behave like entrepreneurs.

Based on thirty-plus years of experience with Fortune 500 companies, small owner-operated businesses and pretty much everything in between, we've developed a proven approach that helps organizations become more cost-competitive in the growing global economy. Today, the biggest decision you will need to make is whether the required shift in leadership philosophy and behavior jibes with your personal belief systems, and whether this commitment is something you're really prepared to make.

Chapter 4
THE BUSINESS MODEL

On May 1, 1996, Southwest Airlines' Flight 1767 departed Las Vegas at 1:00 p.m. for Burbank. As the 737 approached its destination, however, the crew encountered some "irregularities"—the pilot was unable to deploy the left landing gear. That was a problem—a big problem.

To avoid landing the plane on its belly, the pilot decided to perform some stunt maneuvers, hoping to jolt loose the landing gear. The maneuvers were not something most passengers would ever experience, or would want to. So before climbing, diving, and banking at hundreds of miles per hour, the pilot thought it would be wise to tell the passengers about their dilemma and outline what he planned to do about it.

He came over the public address system and (basically) said, "Ladies and gentlemen, this is the captain. We have a problem. We're going to do this and that. I want you to fasten your seatbelts as tightly as possible. Pay very close attention to the flight crew as they come through the cabin. They're going to teach you a crash landing position. I want you *in* that position, and I want you to stay there. I want you to pay attention to the overhead bins. They're going to come open. Things are going to start flying around the cabin, so hang on. This is going to be a *very* rough ride."

I'll bet a million dollars that *nobody* on the plane wanted to hear that news.

I'll bet a billion dollars that every passenger was better off obtaining the knowledge imparted by the captain and flight crew than they would have been without it. If the captain had kept everyone in the dark, I guarantee that every passenger would have jumped to the conclusion that the plane was about to crash. It would have *seemed* like the plane was careening out of control, and that everyone was about to die. In short, it would have been a more terrifying experience than it had to be.

No one liked what was going to happen. No one enjoyed the moment. But all the passengers were able to assume personal control over their own outcomes after getting that information.

As it turned out, the pilot never succeeded in deploying the landing gear, and the plane was diverted to Ontario (CA) where there was a much longer runway. The plane landed (skidded to a stop) safely, and no one was injured. In fact, nobody got as much as a sprained ankle.

This pilot understood something that I've been trying to teach for thirty-plus years—that it's *essential* to move information from the unknown into the known. That's what the Team Development Strategy does. It is a simple, structured, easy-to-follow, cost-efficient, and time-efficient process that helps every staff member know what's happening, where he stands, what's working, and what's not.

Imagine an NBA playoff in which the scoreboard breaks during the fourth quarter. Would that have an impact on the game's outcome? Of course it would! People need performance metrics and results metrics, and that's exactly what the TDS provides.

The TDS is designed to quantify and qualify what was hitherto unknown. It is based on—and supported by—three proprietary software systems, each of which produces quantitative and qualitative reports, numeric data, and comparative data summarized in an easy-to-follow narrative form.

WHY INDIVIDUALS DO
WHAT THEY DO

The Personal Strengths Inventory (PSI) is an online psychometric survey that assesses an individual's motivational interests (what types of work she is motivated to do) and behavioral strengths (how she approaches that work).

In simple layman's language that doesn't require professional training, interpretation, or oversight, the PSI gives users a comparative yardstick that allows:

- Individual employees to validate their own self-perceptions of who they are and what they do well, focusing on their strengths to perform their jobs most successfully.

- Teams of employees to communicate and collaborate more successfully by understanding and appreciating one another's strengths and differences. This helps to reduce both interference and negative judgments about how the person approaches tasks.

- Managers to coach and manage employees individually, based on their individual personalities rather than the conventional approach of treating everyone exactly alike. The Team Covenant makes it permissible to do just that.

The PSI generates self-interpretive reports, supported by online training videos that provide comparative quantitative numeric scales and comparative narrative models, which are its metrics-driven results.

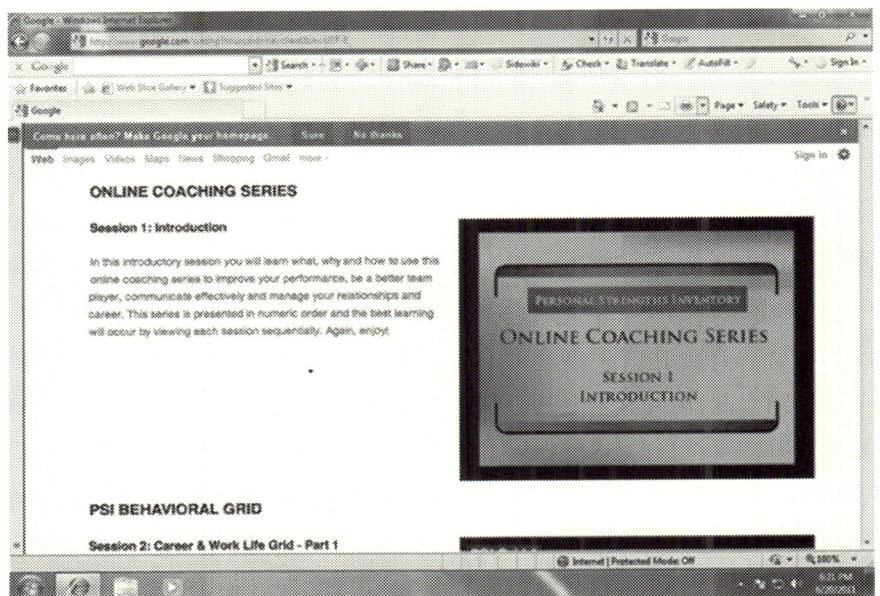

(One of a series of PSI video tutorials at www.teamexcellence.com/training)

The Performance Appraisal and Review System (PARS) is a proprietary, values-based performance appraisal program. It uses the Team Covenant Model as its foundation to evaluate performance against three criteria:

1. Values Competencies—relational and interpersonal performance.

2. Performance Competencies—the knowledge, experience and skills needed for the job.

3. Individual Goals—the specific, quantified goals assigned to each manager and employee.

PARS offers multiple assessment options that can evaluate an employee in the traditional manager-only approach, manager-and-employee approach, or the more contemporary approach called the 360° evaluation (which means individuals evaluate themselves, managers evaluate the employee, and multiple peers and others evaluate the employee), which offers a broader, more objective assessment of performance through many eyes. PARS can process any combination or permutation of these options simultaneously. We developed PARS because there was no off-the-shelf product that would do all of these things against the values-based, Team Covenant model.

PARS produces metrics-driven reports that include a visual summary model of the entire evaluation with a comparative gap-analysis of the various assessment perspectives. It also produces an itemized matrix report of all the individual numeric-scale competency and goal assessments. In addition to individual reports, PARS also generates real-time status reports that let organizations track participation by individuals and departments throughout the performance assessment cycle. PARS also creates summary spreadsheet reports that the organizations can download, where appropriate, into their payroll systems (when PARS is used for compensation considerations). During a review cycle, PARS also sends individuals reminder messages when participants have not completed all of the assigned surveys.

Employee Satisfaction Survey (ESS) is our proprietary, employee surveying program based on the Team Covenant model. The surveys can be customized for each client organization, although most companies use the standard performance survey that we provide. ESS is an annual review of the organization's overall performance and its performance against its Team Covenant commitments through the eyes of employees.

It is completely anonymous, which ensures more objective and honest feedback. It is the "voice" of the employees as they hold the organization accountable. ESS also provides a 24/7/365 online option for anonymous employee input and suggestions throughout the year—the equivalent of an electronic suggestion box.

Finally, ESS produces quantitative, scale-based reports that are segregated numerically by whatever demographic categories the client organization chooses, completing the metrics-driven, organizational-wide accountability model and contract of the Team Covenant.

In summary:

- PSI is the metrics-driven tool that employees use to hold *themselves and one another* accountable for performance and honoring the Team Covenant;

- PARS is the metrics-driven tool that organizations use to hold the *employees* accountable for performance and honoring the Team Covenant; and

- ESS is the metrics-driven tool that employees use to hold the *organization* accountable for performance and honoring the Team Covenant.

Team Development Strategy™ Model

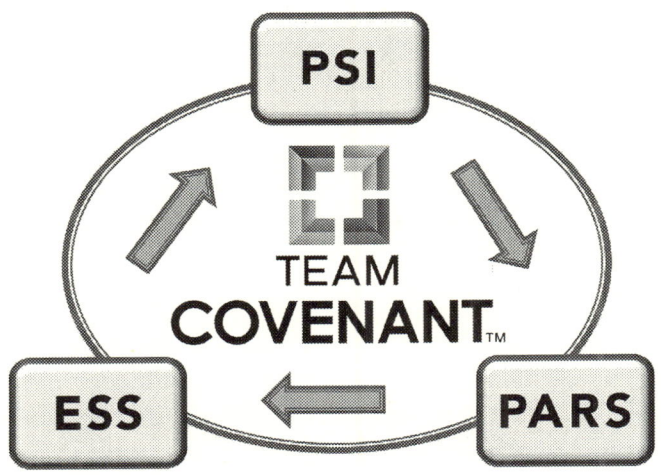

The ultimate purpose of these three tools is to support a philosophy that will motivate every staff member and build trust among every staff member. Please note: Many organizations use various components that they would consider comparable to our system. What's different about our metrics-driven system is that these components are totally integrated, using common language and models. What's more, they are based on a common, well-articulated organization philosophy (the Team Covenant). The TDS develops a level of confidence, trust, and credibility between employees and the organization that cannot be achieved with conventional piecemeal approaches.

Most systems are transactional in nature and in their results TDS is a *transformation* of the client's entire organizational culture.

I'll admit, however, that I am biased—especially when it comes to the PSI. I believe that the PSI provides an easier to interpret, more organizationally functional evaluation than psychometric tests such as the Myers-Briggs, Harrison, and DiSC, among others. The Myers-Briggs (MBTI), for example, begins with a questionnaire that features approximately two hundred questions, and it takes a long time to complete. In addition, the test results cannot be self-administered and interpreted— i.e., you can't conduct the "real deal" without paying an expert to administer it and interpret the results.

The same is true with Personoanalysis; the same is true with Hogan; the same is true with Keirsey. The list is endless. You can't interpret the results yourself unless you have the necessary training because the tests are inevitably esoteric, complex, and subject to a great deal of differing interpretation. This fact, among others, has turned off managers to the necessity and value of psychometric testing for many years. It's probably why some managers would just as soon hire a tarot card reader or an astrologer to analyze their employees' performances and the reasons behind them.

We set out to turn this around. We set out to make industrial psychology something that needn't be feared and loathed—something that laymen can understand and apply immediately. We are continually improving and enhancing our proprietary software so that evaluations and interpretations become even easier—not something for which HR personnel must be specially trained or which require assistance from outside consultants.

We are always working to make our reports better, based on client feedback. No organization needs to pay us $450 an hour to tell them this week what we told them last week, which is what we told them last month and the month before.

Nothing is so esoteric and convoluted that it can't be understood with a little instruction. No member of your staff needs to dedicate thirty years of her life to becoming competent. Our clients become competent in administering and interpreting PSI data immediately. Why? Because the results of our surveys mean *exactly* what they say they mean. You don't have to read between the lines.

Team Excellence designed these products for four key reasons:

1. We *chose* not to impose mandatory/obligatory influence over their application.

2. We *chose* to administer the surveys the way we wanted to, using our philosophy and not the regimentation of the American Psychological Association.

3. We *chose* to use similar language and comparable models in all three evaluations so they made perfect sense in an integrated and cohesive way.

4. We *chose* to make it simple, to skip the psycho-babble, and to free all involved to build their own culture, not ours.

INITIAL IMPLEMENTATION STEPS AT AZ-TECH

Following her review of the Team Covenant, Cheryl Bergen suggested a few changes in order to customize the document for AZ-Tech. Hers were the only revisions put forward, as the other managers seemed to have adopted a "wait and see" attitude—or in Frank's case, an "I'll believe it when I see it" attitude.

Cheryl kept any skepticism to herself. A company veteran who'd risen through the ranks, she was a very bright and caring professional, but she also knew that her HR strengths lay in traditional administrative skills and functions, not strategic HR issues. On paper, the TDS could provide her with the strategic vision and toolbox needed to hurdle the cultural and performance challenges facing the company. In practice, she knew that such programs typically didn't succeed. Still, if the process succeeded, it would give her the "how to" plan and skill set needed to build a more proactive performance management process, so she and her HR Team set about implementing the plan according to the guidelines provided by Team Excellence.

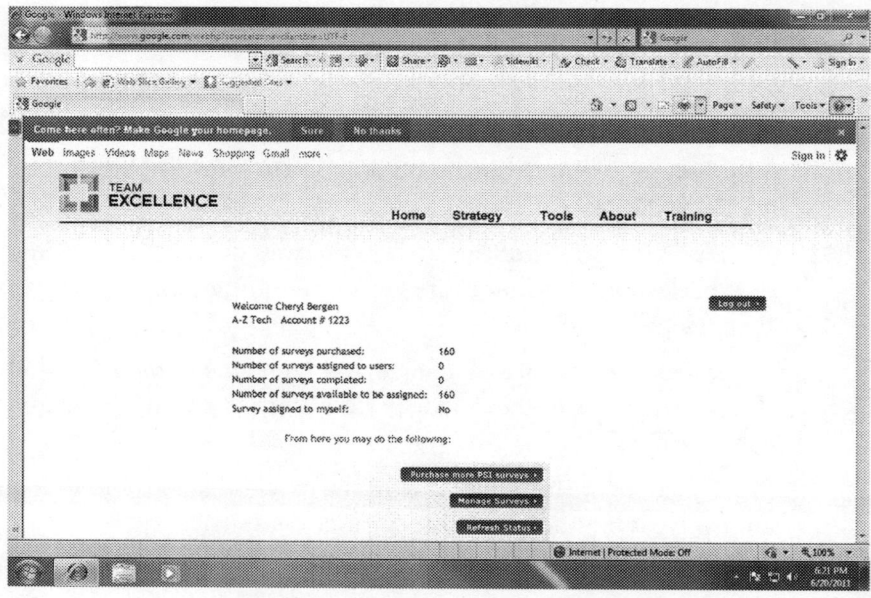

(PSI Company Account Home Page)

First, she set up a discrete and confidential account for administering the PSI through the Team Excellence website, designating herself as the administrator. Then she confirmed that the initial inventory of PSI surveys had been loaded and took the PSI survey to evaluate her own strengths. Next, she familiarized herself with the PSI account management system and previewed the online training support. Finally, she established a prioritized timeline for administering the survey to all 4,600 employees of AZ-Tech and for evaluating the results as they poured in. She even provided a company logo to Team Excellence for inclusion in the Team Covenant and PARS website account.

The process was now ready to be launched.

Chapter 5
EMPLOYEES HOLD THEMSELVES ACCOUNTABLE

Fundamentally, we all believe that we are normal. We believe that the way we think, behave, and respond to different situations and people is the normal way, and that it's how other normal people think and behave. In reality, there's no such thing as "normal." No two people are alike. No two people think and see things exactly the same way, and no two people respond to any situation in the same way.

Unfortunately, we're all very judgmental—even if we publicly withhold those judgments. When *you* say or do something differently from how *I* would, I think that I'm the normal one and you're wrong or abnormal. Twenty-four hours a day, we are subconsciously asking ourselves, "Am I normal?" Most of the time, the resounding answer is "You bet! I'm okay! In fact, if anyone has a problem, it's them, not me!" That's a comical way of describing how we account for individual differences when we don't have a reliable yardstick to use.

PSI *is* a yardstick that's simple and easy to use. It does the two things that organizations hire me to do in the psychometric arena: give people *permission* to be themselves, and help them develop the *tolerance* necessary to "put up" with everyone else.

This is fundamental to making sense of the Team Covenant and creating practical applications for it.

Intuition is the psychological "home base" we all come from. It's our basic personality, our *normal,* our frame of reference that we use in relation to everyone else. It is not our *learned* behavior, which is a template overlay to our intuition, consisting of all the "don't touch hot stoves" behavior we've learned in life. *Intuition* is our basic foundation for making decisions.

The question "who am I" is something all of us ask ourselves from time to time. Our goal is to look at every person's interests, behavior, and motivations in the broader stylistic sense. We want to paint a picture of everyone in the organization and provide an overview of what kind of work-related activities will motivate them the most.

You may already be familiar with the concept of behavior grids. There are a variety of these four-quadrant or four-color grids in use today. But we hope that you will find our model more intuitive and easy to understand—one you can apply more simply, and without a lot of interpretation to your daily thinking and behavior as you use our PSI report to better manage yourself and/or others, make better choices, and improve your communication and relationships with others.

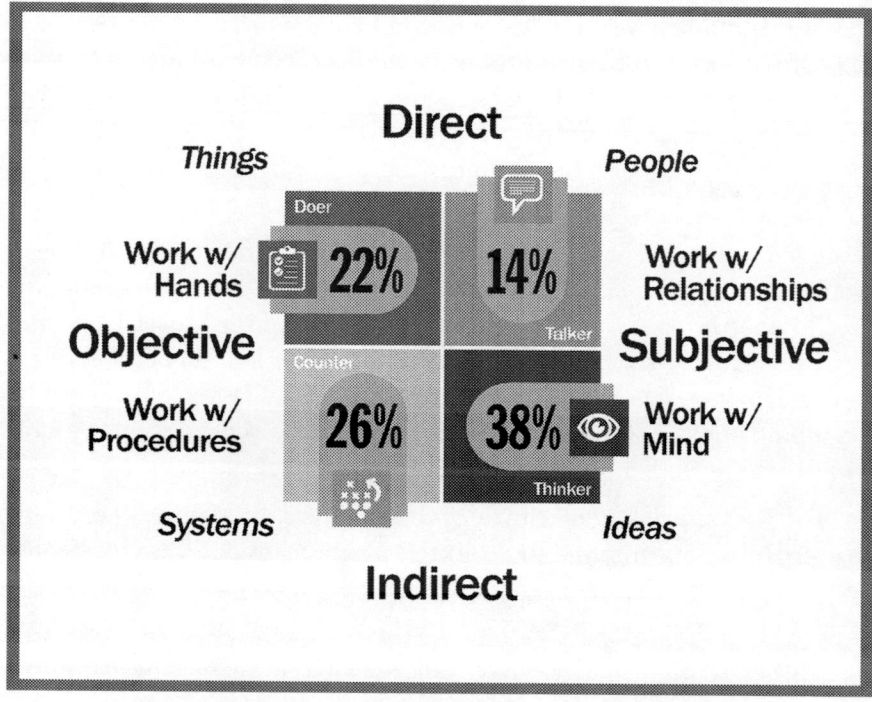

(PSI Presentation of the Hippocratic Model)

THE HIPPOCRATIC MODEL

Hippocrates, known as the father of medicine, was also the father of the four-quadrant grid. About 2,500 years ago, Hippocrates founded the science of psycho-babble when he said, "You can take all the people in the world and put them in one of four categories, and accurately describe how they will behave." For this reason, the model is called the "Hippocratic Model."

The model is based on *opposites*—polar forces and interactive dynamics that are pushing and pulling at one another. What's at the top of the model is the opposite of what's at the bottom. What's over on the left side is the opposite of what's on the right. What's in the upper left hand corner is opposite of what's in the lower right hand corner.

Consider the *vertical axis*, which is a measure of how you present yourself to the world. People at the top are direct, outgoing, extroverted, and engaging. So people at the bottom of this axis are more indirect, soft-spoken, introverted, and reserved. What do introverts think of extroverts and what do extroverts think of introverts? Under stress, extroverts sometimes think that introverts are weak, inept, stupid, and even incompetent. Meanwhile, introverts tend to think extroverts are pushy, brash, overbearing, and obnoxious. And these are some of the more polite descriptive words. None of these assumptions are necessarily true, of course.

Now, let's consider the *horizontal axis*, the left to right dimension. On the left side of the model are the black and white, the tangible, factual, and objective elements of our lives. It *is* or it *isn't*. You can touch it, see it, and grab it. On the right side of the model are all the shades of gray, the subjective, intangible, the intuitive, and abstract—all the human relational and interpersonal factors of life. Each of us possesses every one of these characteristics, but they are combined in a unique style or configuration. To make the model easier to remember, we add color and words to describe the four quadrants in order to gain a better understanding of what the model represents.

In the upper left, Hippocrates said there are *Doers*. These are people who are very hands on and mechanical. They are task-oriented, like to work with things, and like to achieve physical, tangible results. We'll call them blue people.

Hippocrates called the people in the upper right *Talkers*. These people like to motivate and persuade, and influence the thinking and the behavior of other people. Talkers like working with people. We'll call them green people.

In the lower right are the *Thinkers*. These are people who prefer to work conceptually with their minds. They like work that is abstract, conceptual, analytical, and even artistic. These are very creative and innovative people. Let's call them purple people.

And in the lower left are *Counters*. These are people who like to keep track, to work with systems, and to use rules and procedures. They are motivated to initiate and sustain a plan. In short, they like to live and work "by the numbers." These are orange people.

So blue people like to work with their hands, purple people like to work with their minds, green people like to work within relationships, and orange people like to work with and through routines.

All four sets of characteristics can be quite effective, and each individual is a unique and gifted combination of every different style. Let's move ahead to additional definitions that include a more detailed look at the different styles of behavior. We label each of the quadrants with terms that end in the suffix "crat"—as in aristocrat. Based on what we've covered so far, what kind of crat would you expect to find in the upper left quadrant?

How about, autocrat? The autocrat is the person who says, "It needs to be done, so just do it!" A lot of people don't care for autocratic behavior—at least, they think they don't. And I would agree that reactive, overbearing, negative autocratic behavior is inappropriate. But proactive autocratic behavior can be very effective and can even be lifesaving. Autocratic behavior needs to be calm and in control. It needs to be courteous and serve a positive purpose. Autocratic behavior needs to be based on mutual respect and cooperation.

In the upper right, we find the democrat. The democrat says, "Do it, not because I said do it, but because it's in your best interest. Try it; you'll like it. Have I ever lied to you before?" The democrat uses persuasion to gain collaboration, consensus, cooperation, and team effort.

In the lower left is the bureaucrat. The bureaucrat says, "Don't do it because I said do it! Do it because THEY said so. Do it by the numbers; do it by the book. We've been doing it like that around here for the last twenty-seven years. That's the way we do things." The bureaucrat prefers to rely on precedent and proven approaches to ensure things are done correctly.

In the lower right, we find the no crat—the "laissez-faire" individual who disdains structure. The no crat says, "You do things your way, and I'll do things mine. Just leave me alone, and let me do it my way." The no crat prefers his independence, and doesn't want to be made to conform or do things someone else's way.

Here's an example that will help illustrate the four *intuitive styles* in action. We have a room in which there are nine kittens. Problem is, the room is a solid cube. There are no windows or doors, and the task at hand is to get the nine cats out of the room.

The autocrat cuts one hole in the wall and yells "SCAT!" and expects every cat to move instantly. Why? Because he or she said "do it." Do you know anyone like that?

The democrat cuts one hole in the wall and then stands outside the room with a saucer of cream, calling, "Here, kitty, kitty, kitty." She tries to motivate the kittens to leave the room.

The bureaucrat neatly cuts two holes into the wall and meticulously paints "Even" over one hole and "Odd" over the other. She then asks the cats to count off as they pass through the proper holes—one, two, three, four, five… She wants the even-numbered cats to walk through the even-numbered hole, while the odd-numbered cats must pass through the odd-numbered hole. God save the cat that gets out of order!

Finally, the no crat doesn't cut any holes. He stands around for a week, scratching his head, thinking: "Why do we want to get the cats out?" And the cats all die from starvation. Problem solved. That's the laissez-faire approach.

THE CAREER & WORK-LIFE GRID

Note that each of the four quadrants of the grid indicates a percentage of the total grid's value (100 Percent). For most people, one quadrant will represent a larger percentage value than the rest, with the remaining three quadrants decreasing in value by some rank order.

For some of us, there may be two quadrants with an equal (or almost equal) value that are larger than the other two. Either way, you'll quickly see which quadrants most reflect your interests, typical behavior, and motivation, and which quadrants have less influence.

Since personality and behavior are not a simple and single dimension measure of who we are, we've developed the PSI Career & Work-Life Grid to suggest how your interests and behavior are proportionately influenced by every factor that human beings share in common.

We want you to understand that even if one color is far and away the dominant quadrant of your interests and behavior, your personality is also influenced by all the other quadrants. People are not one dimensional beings, but a complex amalgam of strengths—a unique combination of every basic building block. The rank order of your grid colors assesses and provides insights into your interests, as well as the work outcomes that will motivate you and offer the most sustained work and career satisfaction. Knowing these will help you determine where you will most likely develop your best and most productive skills.

Please understand, however, that interests don't imply skills or talent. Liking something and being good at it is not necessarily the same thing. However, there is often a correlation between the two. Most people invest more time and energy in developing skills in activities that they enjoy than those they don't.

If blue (Doer) is your largest grid quadrant, you want to do work that is hands on, here and now, work that produces tangible, task-oriented results. You like work that is physical, and may literally like to work with your hands. You probably enjoy mechanical and/or operational activities, and like results that you can see, touch, and feel. You will find satisfaction in implementing and initiating work and tasks. You have a high sense of urgency and want to finish results now. You like practical, here-and-now solutions; and patience may not be your greatest virtue. You will typically like group activities that apply clear-cut data. You will prefer a busy schedule, and are prone to be direct with others and logical in your thinking and decision making.

If green (Talker) is your largest grid quadrant, you want work that involves human relationships and influencing other people. That's not just in the sales profession. It's any work that involves working with other people and is measured in relationships, which includes teaching, preaching, consulting, politics, and any other people-focused activity. You find satisfaction in sharing and promoting ideas and causes. You are motivated to persuade and influence the thinking and actions of others and to have an impact on what they choose to do. Your sense of urgency is also high, and you may not have as much patience as you need sometimes. You will typically like activities that offer an opportunity to be competitive and assertive. You prefer to be flexible, and you want to incorporate a certain amount of novelty and variety into your thinking and decision-making.

If purple (Thinker) is your largest grid quadrant, you like working with your mind. You seek work that has analytical, conceptual, creative, and maybe artistic outcomes. You want results that improve the future because you are a planner. Your career choices might include jobs in academics, research, engineering, programming, and the arts. You find satisfaction figuring things out and dealing with concepts. You are motivated to find abstract solutions, and you sometimes want to be allowed to work on your own, without having to meet the expectations of others. Your level of urgency is driven more by preparing for the future and finding new and better ways to get things done. This means that you may sometimes put off things, hoping to figure out how to make them even better. You will probably like activities that offer you opportunities for individualized support and allow you to express your feelings. You do not want to be rushed. You like time to reflect on your thinking and decision making, so sometimes you may be more engaged in your feelings than appropriate or productive.

If orange (Counter) is your largest grid quadrant, you want work that is measured... in measurements. You want outcomes that result from systems, procedures, and implementing plans. You enjoy numbers, processes, and things that you can count and track. Fields of interest might include accounting, finance, computers, and any systems-oriented activities. You find satisfaction in scheduling and initiating work that involves detail. You have a high desire to control the outcome of your effort. You like practical and objective results, so being sensitive to others around you is not your greatest strength. Sometimes you will want such perfection that it can be hard to please you or meet your expectations. You typically can be counted on to be organized and highly focused. You place great importance on being able to trust others. And we can count on you to be consistent and predictable in your thinking and decision making.

TEAM
EXCELLENCE

John Smith
REPORT NUMBER: PSI00000000
REPORT DATE: 05/10/2014

Career & Work-Life Grid Report

Your Report Results

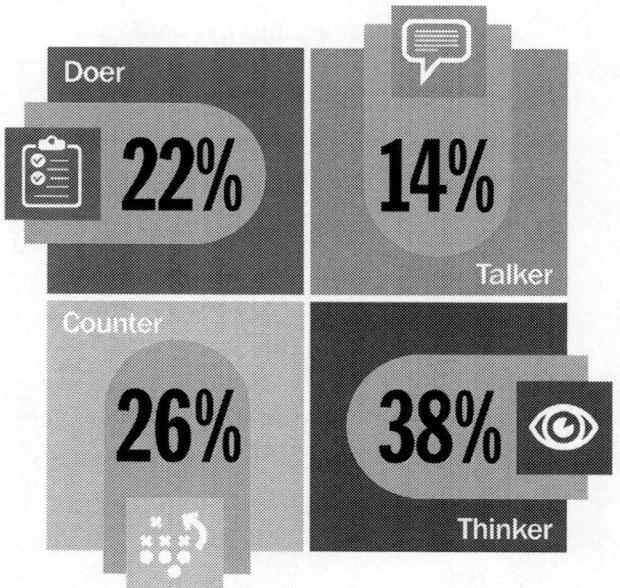

Grid Report Summary

It is important to understand that you are a very unique and exceptional combination of all the preferences and behaviors presented on this Career & Work-Life Grid; yet everyone leans more one way or the other. The areas of the Grid where you are the strongest are your predominant strengths and they will typically be those areas in which you most easily excel and develop skills. Your strengths are what motivate and create drive within you. Those other areas, where you are not as strong, are not necessarily a weakness, but they may represent a bias on your part that can limit what you ultimately achieve. Think of the Grid as a series of filters through which you view your world. The value of this improved self-knowledge is the ability to capitalize on your strengths without letting your biases stand in your way.

© Team Excellence, Inc. All rights reserved.

(Career & Work-Life Grid Model)

The rest of an individual's PSI report is presented in a series of graphic and written measures called behavioral dashboards. The dashboards present a series of important but contrasting behavioral scales—that measure one approach to a specific behavior versus an opposite approach. The dashboard quickly and simply defines intuitive behavior in dealing with common situations, as well as interpersonal relationships, measuring behavior in seven separate categories. Each dashboard offers significant insight into the individual's personality and preferred style.

The dashboards are *not* an indication of "best behaviors." There is no *best behavior*. Remember, the Personal Strengths Inventory IS NOT a test, but a comparative survey. Every behavior can be positive, if applied in a positive and proactive manner.

Conversely, behaviors generally considered "positive" can get in the way if they are applied inappropriately and reactively.

Proactive behavior means that you're in control and choosing to "make things happen." Reactive behavior means that you're merely responding to events as they happen. The most important thing is determining which behavior is best in any given situation, and why a particular behavior may not occur to you intuitively and require instead that you make a conscious choice.

Can you pick and choose your behavior? Absolutely! That's the whole point of the PSI process. Your Personal Strengths Inventory is not a horoscope which states that "this is who you are, and sorry, but there's nothing you can do to change." The PSI reveals your intuitive behavioral styles and preferences. By knowing your intuitive strengths, you can learn when to apply them and when you can choose to behave differently if the situation demands it. If we did not have choice over our behavior, what would be the value of an assessment tool such as the PSI?

Each dashboard shows you which way you lean on a given behavioral scale, and like a speedometer, it tells you "how fast" or "how slow" you typically go. By lending clear definition to your strengths, and pointing out a contrasting and complementary approach, you can "throttle up" or "apply the brakes" as needed. Think of it as a mind game that can help you develop new skills. As with any skill, proficiency requires repetitive practice.

WORKING WITH OTHERS

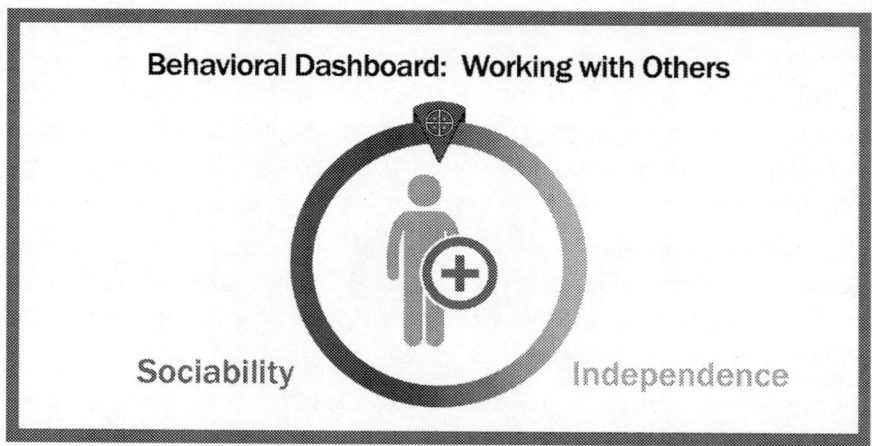

The first dashboard is "Working with Others." It measures how we work with and socialize in groups. Do you like to work by yourself or in small groups? Do you prefer to work in large groups, getting people to participate and build consensus?

If your "Sociability" score is high, you're probably a very outgoing person. You meet and greet easily. You make good first impressions, and are most effective when you're with and around other people. You are good at building consensus, and it's important for you to get people to join in and belong. You like meetings and group activities, and you not only keep your door open, but are usually the one standing in everybody else's door.

One on-the-job implication is that many people will defer to your outgoing style and will take a back seat. When the team or group needs to hear everyone's point of view, you may sometimes need to deliberately play a quieter role.

If your "Independence" score is high, your strength is self-sufficiency, and you're good at working alone or in small groups. You're probably a reserved person who values your privacy. In general, you don't behave in an outgoing way. You want to fit in and belong, and you don't mind coming to staff meetings—preferably no more than once a year (just teasing). You want to know what is expected of you and then be left alone to get the work done. Other people may think you're a little shy or aloof because if you have an office with a door, you prefer to keep it closed.

An on-the-job implication is that others may question your commitment and enthusiasm for the team's goals and agenda. Try to openly express your commitment and interest more often.

If your score is more moderate, you may be quite engaging, gracious, and outgoing—most of the time. But in your mind, you really value time alone, when you don't have to please people or live up to their expectations. My wife, Carolyn, is like this. Carolyn is very friendly and outgoing. She's a great hostess, and she seems very comfortable in other people's presence. But her idea of a great Friday night is a book, a glass of wine, and a very quiet setting, which sometimes involves getting me out of the house. People like this can be socially selective—picking and choosing relationships very carefully and limiting close friendships to a relative handful.

One on-the-job implication is that (again), you are intuitively more comfortable with a select group of people. You gravitate toward some people more intuitively than others and may rely on those relationships more. Unintentionally, you may appear to have a clique of trusted friends, causing some people to feel excluded. You need to pay special attention to including everyone more often.

DEALING WITH CHANGE

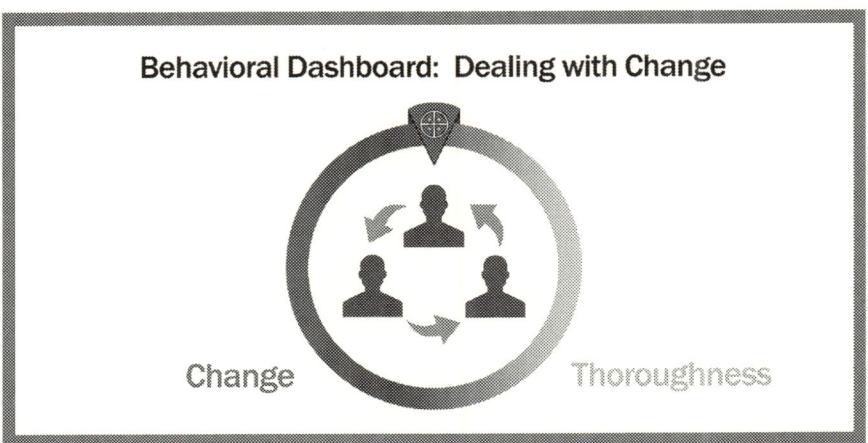

The second dashboard is "Dealing with Change." It measures our preferences for change and variety versus thoroughness. In the event that you've been marooned on a desert isle for the last few decades, the business world is changing at an accelerated pace.

How we apply our resources and time is changing dramatically: we need to get more done with less; be more sensitive and tolerant of others, become more self-sufficient, and personally accountable for what we accomplish.

If your "Change" score is high, you prefer variety and a lot of simultaneous activity. You enjoy spontaneity with your variety, and can get bored pretty easily if you're forced into a routine. You like new approaches and methods, and yet you deal fairly well with the unexpected. You look for new things to do and are pretty effective at multitasking.

On-the-job implications are that you may be juggling too many projects simultaneously, causing others to lose confidence in your ability to deliver everything promised. Work on establishing the right set of priorities and then compromise by limiting the total number of things you tackle all at once.

If your "Thoroughness" score is high, you like thoroughness and consistency. You are good at concentrating attention and staying focused on tasks and priorities. You want and need advance notice when something is about to change, or when something new is going to be added to your plate. You like to finish things and check them off your list.

Look ahead at your "Action" score in Your Preferred Pace dashboard. If you have high "Action" score with this high "Thoroughness" score, you REALLY love to finish things. You'll stay until midnight, if needed, to complete important tasks. If both scores are high, you'll stand around for another hour or two once you're done to admire what you just accomplished.

An on-the-job implication is that you may appear to be unwilling to participate in inevitable changes. Show more enthusiasm for new or novel ways to improve work, and manage your intuitive resistance to the unexpected.

If your score is more Moderate but leans toward the Change side, you probably behave in a flexible way, handle the unexpected pretty well, and like to do lots of different things. However, you need to know when the really big things in your life are going to change. You don't like big surprises.

The potential on-the-job implication is that you occasionally lose the strength of your routine flexibility and seem to get stuck in the mud. When you feel pressured with too many surprises or new things, acknowledge your uneasiness, and ask for assistance from your manager or a trusted colleague.

If your score is more Moderate but leans toward the "Thoroughness" side of the dashboard, you may be fairly consistent and thorough on the outside but really *do* like novelty and variety. You need opportunities to try new things, and you can also get bored with too much routine.

A potential on-the-job implication is that you sometimes appear erratic in your work habits compared to your normal orderly self. Watch for moments when you go in too many different directions, and try to manage priorities more carefully.

YOUR PREFERRED PACE

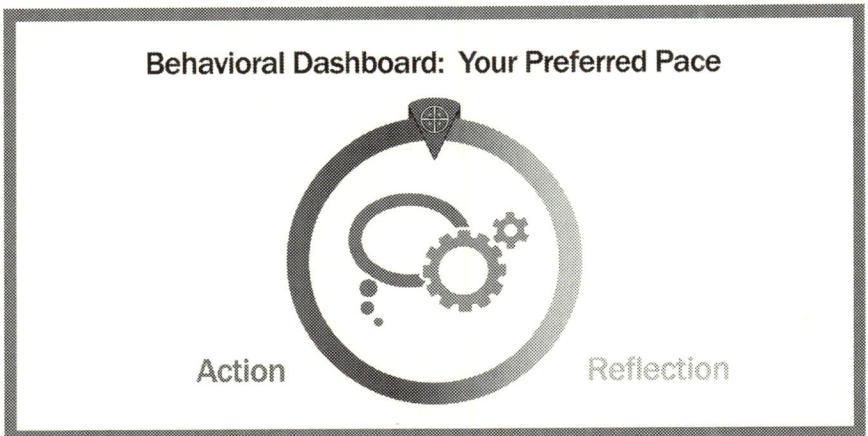

The third dashboard is "Your Preferred Pace." It measures our sense of energy. Do you like to move fast? Do you have a great sense of urgency about most things? This dashboard also measures preferred pace for action versus reflection—your preference for physical activity or reflective activity. Are you a very direct, action-oriented person? Do you like to keep physically busy, and do you work hard and play hard?

Or do you prefer a slower and more reflective approach? Do you like to figure things out before you start a project, and is efficiency of energy an important consideration for you?

If your "Action" score is high, you are a very action-oriented person. You always need to be doing something constructive, and you don't do rest very well! You have a great sense of urgency, are always willing to tackle a new project because you probably have energy to burn, like quick results, and measure success in immediate results. Your strength is that you can often pull off being a *super-doer*, and always have something to show for it.

One on-the-job implication is that you can be a workaholic, lacking patience with both processes and other people—and I'm being polite. Show your manager and coworkers that you value balance and respect their approach to getting things done.

If your "Reflection" score is high, you prefer to think things through and get them done right the very first time. You want personal control over your schedule and responsibilities and prefer to have sufficient time to reflect before taking action.

Your strength is that you're a deliberate person and prefer thoroughness over quick results. Usually, you are a very careful and cautious person.

One on-the-job implication, especially if your scores are very high, is that your manager and fellow team members may see you as lethargic and lacking ambition. This can be a critical issue because you may well be *the most* motivated person in the whole company, but prefer to live your life at a different pace.

Pay careful attention to demonstrating urgency more often. Don't let people assume that you don't care.

If your score is more Moderate, you may be active and busy most of the time. You have a moderate sense of urgency and like to get a great deal done. But you may need to manage your energy sometimes, calling a "time out" to recharge your batteries. You tend to work, work, work, and then stop and rest for a while. On occasion, you may even run out of gas.

An on-the-job implication—a *potential* implication—is that others may see you working in spurts of energy, because you *do* need to call "time outs." Be proactive about keeping your manager and fellow workers posted on the status of projects, so they don't misperceive you as leaving things unattended.

These days, it's common for people to claim that they "just don't have enough time" to do everything they need to do in their personal and professional lives (even if you *think* you have time, news and advertisements are always claiming that you don't, because of "today's busy lifestyles").

The truth is each of us has all the time there is. There is no more. The real issue is learning how to use time differently—more effectively. If you're doing everything the way you did five years ago, you're probably in trouble, and things are only going to get worse.

We have to learn how to use time better, and that means making better choices. To determine how to be more responsible for managing your time, accountabilities, and pace, use the behavioral dashboard.

YOUR PERSONAL IDENTITY

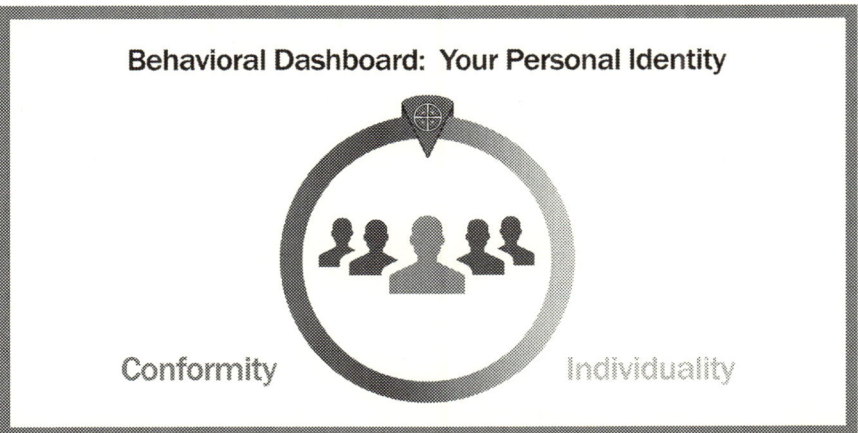

The fourth dashboard is "Your Personal Identity." It measures your self-identity and personal values. All of us have a sense of personal identity—of who *we are* when compared to others. It's connected to our self-worth and self-esteem. Your personal identity is a measure of your individuality and personal independence. Are you a person who understands what most people think, or are you more individualistic in your way of thinking?

If your "Conformity" score is high, you think you *know* what most people think. Guess what? You're correct much of the time! People with a high conformity score often have an intuitive understanding of what others think.

If that's you, you like tradition and appreciate the conventional approach to getting things done. You love hot dogs, Chevrolets, motherhood, the flag, and apple pie. I'm not saying you are more patriotic than the rest of us, but you really *do* value traditional things. You prefer a predictable environment and like to fit in.

One on-the-job implication is that you may appear to overconform on the big issues. So evaluate more carefully how you feel about important job and work-related issues. Consider whether you have an opinion different from the majority and whether that opinion deserves stronger expression from time to time.

If your "Individuality" score is high, you're a real free spirit. You like doing things through a unique and individualistic approach. You need frequent opportunities to stand out and be different. You want to fit in and belong, but you want to be appreciated for bringing something special to the dance.

An on-the-job implication is that you may seem to always need to do things *your way*, possibly in opposition to others. You and everyone around you will be well served if you work on the art of compromise and take satisfaction in getting things done through greater consensus and collaboration.

If your score is more Moderate, leaning toward "Conformity," you typically behave in a conventional way most of the time, but you may need to be valued for your uniqueness (on occasion), and really don't want to be pigeonholed with the rest of us.

One on-the-job implication is that on those occasions, you may appear to be rebellious. It's okay to have strong and passionate opinions, but you can also benefit from working on the art of compromise.

If your score is more Moderate but leaning toward "Individuality," you're a free thinker (most of the time) when it comes to expressing yourself. You can certainly stand up for what you believe, but you may need assurance that you *do* belong—that you are a part of "us." You have a need and appreciation for the conventional, more traditional approaches to life.

An on-the-job implication is that you can lose your typical self-sufficient attitude, and resort to conformity when others think you should stand up for what you believe. Work on achieving the right balance of independent thinking and group compromise, and ask for feedback about your ideas and contributions.

Here are some ideas from which we can all benefit—no matter what our scores. On the job, most of us believe that we *should know* precisely what to do. We think the boss expects that we do know what to do. Otherwise, we wouldn't have been given the job. Right? So we protect ourselves and our positions by frequently pretending that we know exactly what to do—even when we don't have a clue. Anything else would be political and career suicide.

Here's the rub. Today, too much change is occurring for any one person to keep up with all of it. Nobody can possibly know how to do everything. Wouldn't it be something if we all could learn to say, "I hadn't really thought about it like that. Maybe I'm wrong, maybe you're right." Isn't that a novel idea? We all need to learn to do this, but under stress, it can be extremely difficult. This makes accepting accountability even tougher on some occasions.

ASSERTING YOURSELF

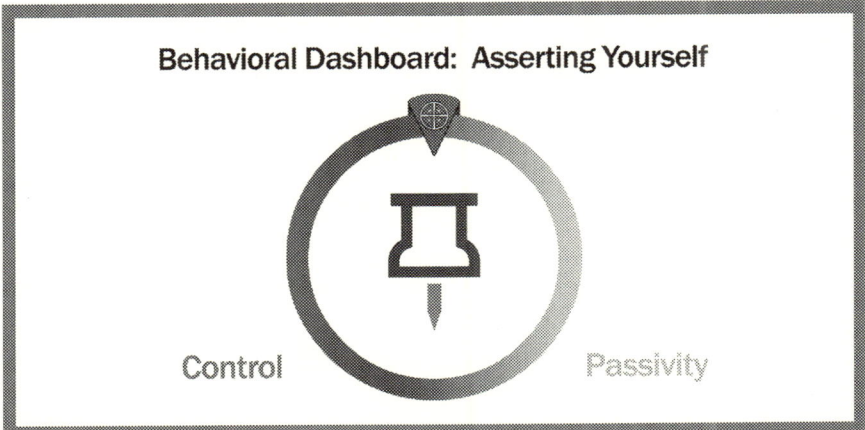

Behavioral Dashboard: Asserting Yourself

Control   Passivity

The fifth dashboard is "Asserting Yourself." It measures your level of comfort with authority and control. How you deal with authority and control affects your working relationships. It's also one of the most critical factors influencing the amount of trust established between people. This factor has an almost invisible and intuitive impact on how much trust we give and receive. Let's examine how we assert ourselves.

If your "Control" score is high, you prefer a direct and assertive approach to getting things done. You respect authority, and want to know who's in charge. If you were an army colonel, you'd expect junior officers and enlisted personnel to salute you, and you would have no problem saluting all of the generals! Authority goes in both directions.

You value a clearly defined chain of command. Your life philosophy is something like, "If we don't tell those rascals what to do, it just won't get done." You don't necessarily look for confrontation, but you address things head on—one of your great strengths. And high control is a part of being competitive.

An on-the-job implication is that some people feel intimidated by your directness and will choose to back away. What *you* see as direct, *they* see as confrontational. This can limit the collaboration you achieve with others, so I recommend that you learn to put question marks at the end of your sentences, rather than periods or exclamation points! Spend more time *asking*, rather than *telling* people what needs to be done.

If your "Passivity" score is high, you prefer to approach life in a more indirect way. You don't like conflict and confrontation. In fact, you hate it. You want to ask others and be asked yourself. You don't like having demands placed on you, and you don't demand things of others. Your life philosophy is something like, "People ought to do what people ought to do. They should simply do things because they're supposed to do them, and not because we make them." Most of the time, you're not a demanding person, and you exercise authority in a low-key way, which is one of your great strengths.

One on-the-job implication is that you avoid dealing with uncomfortable issues until—sometimes—they boil over into a crisis. Others may perceive this as a weakness. Develop the discipline to address problems when they first occur to prevent small problems from becoming big ones.

If your score is more Moderate and leaning toward "Control," it means that you're moderately direct and assertive most of the time, but you'll behave in a low key and easygoing manner until things aren't working out. Then you'll assert yourself more than people probably expect, which is a polite way of saying that you may get more demanding and even exhibit an explosive temper when things don't go smoothly.

One on-the-job implication is that you may appear more low-key about various issues than you really are. Speak up more often and earlier about what you believe and think needs to happen. Be more proactive about expressing your point of view.

If your score is more Moderate and leaning toward "Passivity," you prefer a low-key, non-confrontational approach, and you don't want to be controlled by anyone else. What often happens is that you may avoid addressing problems head on until they've morphed into a "big deal." When you do address them, you don't do it well. You can become explosive, even nuclear, because you've traveled so far outside your comfort zone that your skills and confidence don't serve anyone very well, especially you.

An on-the-job implication is that you may appear so low-key that you scare the guacamole out of colleagues when you have a bad hair day. You can shock and awe people with your unexpected "surge" in behavior. Again, the solution is to tackle problems while they're small enough to be more easily managed.

As I mentioned earlier, this behavioral factor significantly influences how we establish and sustain trust in relationships. There's something almost "chemical" about how it works. *High-control people* don't feel confidence in high passivity people. There's a suspicion that they are not strong enough or trustworthy. Meanwhile, high passivity people don't feel comfortable around high-control people. They feel uncomfortable and intimidated.

Experience demonstrates that people need to use question marks as often as possible at the ends of sentences. They work much better to gain people's cooperation and trust—no matter what might be considered the preferred approach to communications and work.

EXPRESSING YOUR FEELINGS

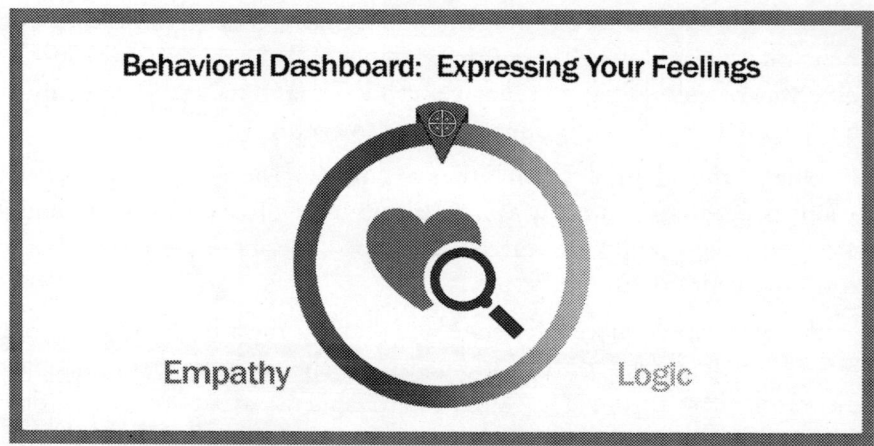

The sixth dashboard is "Expressing Your Feelings." It measures how you express your feelings and how you reveal that you care. We all care. Do you want to do a good job? Do you want to be a good employee or good manager? Do you want to be a good spouse or parent? Do you want to be a good person, or a good citizen? Do you care?

If your "Empathy" score is high, you are a very expressive person. You show us your care and feelings easily and openly. You are sympathetic and warm in your behavior, and you need to be given opportunities to demonstrate your feelings and concern about important, subjective issues.

If you max out this scale, you have this invisible beacon on your forehead that's radiating a signal twenty-four hours a day, seven days a week: I care! I CARE! People probably confide their deepest, darkest secrets to you, and you may wonder why they tell you all this stuff. They're telling you because they intuitively know that you really do care.

One on-the-job implication is that you may be perceived as *too* expressive with your feelings. People will sometimes think that you lack necessary objectivity. Don't suppress your feelings but be more aware of how and when you share them. Balance emotional expressions with an appropriate focus on demonstrating your business savvy.

If your "Logic" score is high, you may be one of those stoic "triage nurses" in our lives. You're the person we rely on to save us in a crisis. You are logical, objective, and can detach your feelings more easily from situations that require an unemotional response. You're the person who first calls the police when there's been an accident.

You make sure a sufficient number of ambulances have been requested. You assign passersby to direct traffic so that nobody else gets hurt.

An on-the-job implication is that you may not show enough interest and empathy to your fellow workers, manager, or even some customers. Work on acknowledging others' feelings as well as your own and develop more comfort in expressing how you feel about things... from time to time.

If you have a Moderate score that leans toward "Empathy," you will be fairly open in expressing your feelings but may push back when there is an absence of logical thinking in the room. Work on finding the right balance between showing your feelings to others and engaging them in pursuit of logical solutions to problems or challenges.

One on-the-job implication is that others may not understand the logic that you apply to your critical thinking and may not have as much confidence in your positions as they would if they only understood that internal logic. Be proactive about sharing how you arrive at conclusions. Don't assume that people will know this automatically.

If you have a more Moderate score that leans toward "Logic," you are typically logical, sequential, and relatively detached in your outward behavior. But inside, you may be more feeling-oriented than people realize. You actually have a greater capacity for understanding and experiencing emotional issues than you reveal. You may need opportunities to express and deal with your feelings, but people may not offer you the opportunities (or respond to them) because they observe only your *external* logical, routine, and unemotional behavior.

One on-the-job implication is that your typical attitude doesn't adequately express the genuine empathy that you often feel. You should develop a more routine expression of interest and empathy for others.

ATTENTION TO DETAIL

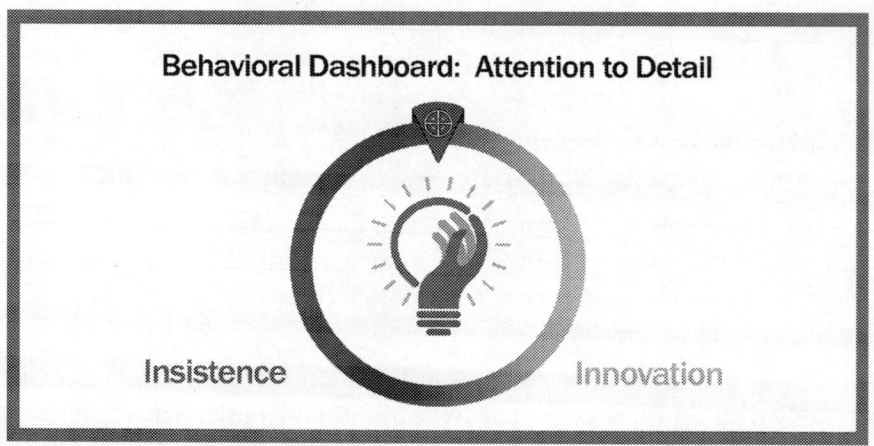

The seventh and last dashboard is "Attention to Detail." It is a measure of your *insistence* and how you routinely deal with systems, procedures, and detail. Are you organized and structured? Are you punctual and take a best-practices approach to almost everything? Or are you better at being flexible and willing to try new ways of doing things? Are you very concerned with how others get things done? Or do you just want those things done well?

If your "Insistence" score is high, you are a very organized, precise, and almost always punctual human being. You like to get things done in an orderly manner. You love sequence and would prefer that most everything be done exactly right. You want and need detail and don't like leaving things to chance. It's always better to have a specific plan, and life is best when that plan is followed and if your "Insistence" score is very high, followed exactly to the letter. Your strength is that there is no ambiguity. People always know what you want and how you would like things done.

One on-the-job implication is that you may give people more information that they can process. When they ask for the time, you tell them how to build a watch. Give people information in smaller doses, and check for feedback. Ask them, intermittently, have I given you enough information, or do you want more?

If your "Innovation" score is high, you are a very flexible and a hard-to-rattle person when things don't go according to plan. You handle the unscheduled and unplanned very easily and (usually) quite well. Also, you enjoy figuring out new ways to get things done. In fact, you don't like doing things the same old way again and again.

You prefer to think of plans as general guidelines and suggestions. You like to know what the end goal is, but you want to fill in the blanks on your own. Your strength is allowing other people great latitude in accomplishing their responsibilities. They can take a bus, a plane, a train, a car, a boat, or a horse. You don't really care as long as they end up *where* you want them *when* you need them to be there.

One on-the-job implication is that when you think you've been very specific, some people will have heard you speak in *general* terms. You would also do well to ask others if you've provided them with enough information.

If your score is Moderate and leaning toward "Insistence," you are usually quite organized and orderly in how you accomplish tasks, but you want and need a fair amount of discretion on how to get things done. What you're really saying is, "I'll be very organized, punctual, and dependable, but please don't tell me how to do it! Let me create my own details." For most of your life, you've thought, "Do they think I'm stupid? I could have figured that out by myself."

An on-the-job implication is that you may resist imposed detail and appear less cooperative than you intend to be. Try listening more carefully to fully understand instructions and information without giving the impression that you already know what someone is about to say.

If your score is Moderate, but leaning toward "Innovation," you show good flexibility and an easygoing nature most of the time, but you need clear and specific information and a well-defined understanding of what you're expected to do. You may feel a lot of ambiguity in certain situations because other people may assume you don't want lots of detailed information. Consequently, on occasion, you may need to be more direct and ask exactly what your managers or colleagues need you to do.

One on-the-job implication is that it may seem that you don't want as much information as you actually want and need. Ask for more detail if you're not sure what was just said or what you need to do.

Here's a tip that works for everyone, no matter which way they lean on the behavioral dashboard. When providing information, conducting a meeting, assigning a project to someone else, or in any situation where detailed instructions should be confirmed, say: "I need your help." When we tell people that we need their help, most want to give it. What you're really saying is that you need an agreement, and most people are willing to enter into an agreement and offer assistance when they're asked.

This is a better and more productive approach than what's usually done in the business world which is to state, "Are we clear" or "Do you know what to do?" People tend to say yes, even if they have no idea, because they don't want to appear incompetent or dimwitted, especially if you happen to be the boss. The assumed risk is too high.

The second thing you should say is, "Help me make sure I've done my part correctly." This implies that if there's a misunderstanding or lack of clarity, it's not *their* fault but yours. You subtract any hint of accusation from the equation and gain allies willing to contribute to achieving shared solutions. Collaboration is always better than compliance. Collaboration lasts. Compliance is usually short lived.

The third thing you should say is, "Tell me how you're going to accomplish what we've just agreed to." Now is the time to determine if people truly understood the information or instructions. It's better to catch any misunderstandings here than to learn that nobody understood you a month later… when you're about to miss a deadline. If you want a subordinate to travel to Los Angeles, make sure he understands that… and doesn't hop on a plane to Miami.

IMPLEMENTING THE TDS

Cheryl Bergen had never been busier.

To pave the way for implementation of the Team Development Strategy and Team Covenant, and to gain employee and management buy-in, she and her team had devoted countless hours to identifying individual and group participants for TDS orientation sessions; she'd scheduled dates, times, and locations for the sessions in tandem with Team Excellence and had issued company-wide announcements in advance.

In addition, she'd prepared appropriate remarks for Colin to introduce the sessions at some of AZ-Tech's locations and prepared detailed FAQ sheets to respond to employee inquiries. Finally, she'd made the arrangements for the meeting facilities where the sessions would be conducted and supervised the meetings herself.

She'd also developed a structure and timeframe for ongoing new-employee training, which centered on a PowerPoint presentation supplied by Team Excellence. That was only the beginning. Over the next few months, she needed to build behavioral *accountability* in the workforce by integrating the PSI, PARS, and ESS into an ongoing organizational process. For the PSI implementation alone, she'd need to:

- Determine if Team Excellence's online PSI tutorial videos could meet the individual and team training requirements for AZ-Tech. Based on internal needs and managers' existing levels of interpersonal awareness and skill, she could choose from the following options for PSI training:

1. Online videos as the sole training resource.

2. Online videos for individual introduction to the PSI, followed up by manager-led team meetings in which they conducted team development discussions.

3. Online videos for individual introduction to the PSI training programs followed up by Team Excellence-led meetings for some teams in the company.

4. Have Team Excellence conduct the initial PSI training and then use the online videos to provide follow-up and ongoing reinforcement training.

5. Have Team Excellence train the managers who would then lead PSI training sessions for their respective staffs.

Cheryl was leaning toward a hybrid of the last two options. Though she was satisfied that the online videos could (in theory) serve as the sole training source, experience had taught her that trained in-house managers would be better suited for tackling unexpected questions and problems. They'd be able to translate the whole process into a company-specific and even team-specific context, which would help employees recognize its practical value. As long as the managers bought into the new system and accepted ownership for success, they could prove invaluable in helping everyone see the workaday "ground floor" benefits of the Team Covenant and TDS. That way they would not view the system as some experimental academic theory on how organizations and employees can improve performance and accountability.

In other words, these managers could inspire subordinates with a "factory floor-level" vision of how the TDS will improve their lives and career trajectories and work to dispel any cynicism that the program was just window dressing. *That* was Phase 1 of the TDS implementation. In Phase 2, she would have to:

- Develop an appropriate training strategy (or strategies) to implement the PSI training throughout the organization.

- Send organizational-wide announcements about the implementation of TDS Phase 2, reminding the staff of the behavioral accountability within the Team Covenant, and outlining the projected roll-out steps, timetable and schedule.

- Deploy PSI survey assignments to all managers and employees.

- Track PSI survey completions and follow up to ensure that the surveys were completed in a timely fashion.

- Conduct initial PSI training.

- Meet with managers to determine overall response to the initial PSI training, focus on recurring use of PSI reports in managers' coaching efforts for employees, and determine further training needs for managers in using PSI.

- Conduct small group discussions with employees as a follow-up to initial PSI training, and solicit feedback for understanding opportunities to use the PSI reports in daily work.

- Develop a structure and timeframe for conducting ongoing training reinforcement.

- Develop PSI team reports and determine the appropriate utilization strategy.

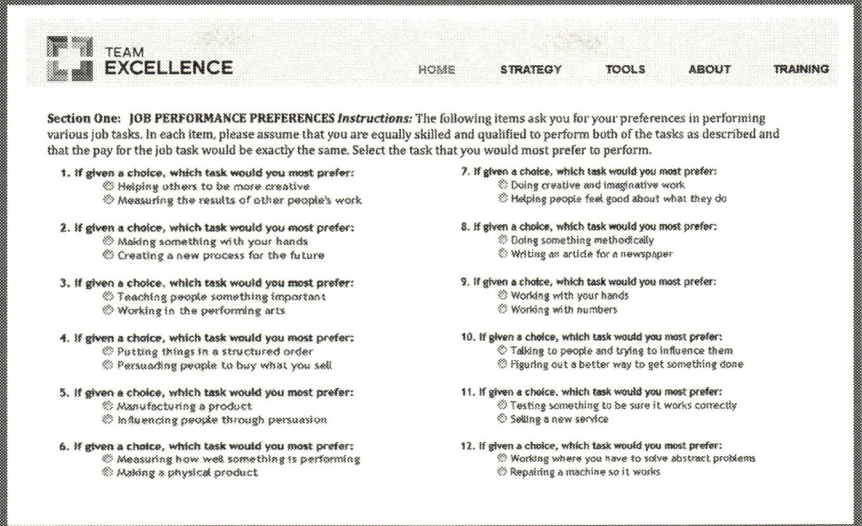

(Sample PSI Survey Items)

Despite her increased work volume, the process was not without its rewards. Cheryl was impressed with the insights gleaned from her own PSI evaluation. Of course, most of the information reinforced what she'd already known about her personal strengths and work preferences. But she was delighted with how succinctly the data was presented both graphically and in written summaries.

Reading the reports about herself and her fellow managers was more like reading a short background profile prepared by an "empathetic" FBI agent, rather than something written in code, which required an expert to interpret.

In each report, the total PSI picture was right there in front of her, and no assembly was required.

For example, the four-quadrant, four-color grid instantly identified Cheryl as being primarily a Counter (Orange) in terms of preferences and behaviors, and secondarily a Thinker (purple). It was a combination well suited to her position.

As a Counter, she was a procedure-oriented person who liked to establish systems and processes, and work within established approaches. She'd always been motivated by specific and detailed plans, and liked to rely on precedent to guide her actions.

At the same time, she enjoyed work that was conceptual and analytical. She was highly motivated by innovative plans for the future—plans like those surrounding implementation of the Team Development Strategy. This explained why she tended to be outgoing and personable one day, and the next day behaved like a hermit, locking herself in her office to focus on inventing new procedures or policies.

She especially liked the tone of the PSI reports. She was sure the tone would be more palatable to the average manager and employee than those of other psychometric tests. For one thing, the PSI reports characterized behavioral preferences and styles as *strengths*, instead of "strengths and weaknesses."

This might seem like a small difference, but even nonpsychologists can tell you that people like to have "positive spins" on their personalities and world views. They'd rather be told, "Here are the strengths with which you've been blessed, and here are the areas in which you need work," rather than "You're a good communicator, but you suck at details!"

The fact that Cheryl was not a natural "people person" *could* be characterized as a "weakness" for someone in her profession. But as she knew, this "weakness" was something she'd worked hard to strengthen during her career, and she'd reached the point where interpersonal relationships *seemed* to come naturally—at least to her peers. Only her friends and family knew that she was naturally shy.

Cheryl's Career & Work-Life Grid is on the next page.

TEAM
EXCELLENÇE

Cheryl Bergen
REPORT NUMBER: PSI68565308
REPORT DATE: 06/25/2014

Career & Work-Life Grid Report

Your Report Results

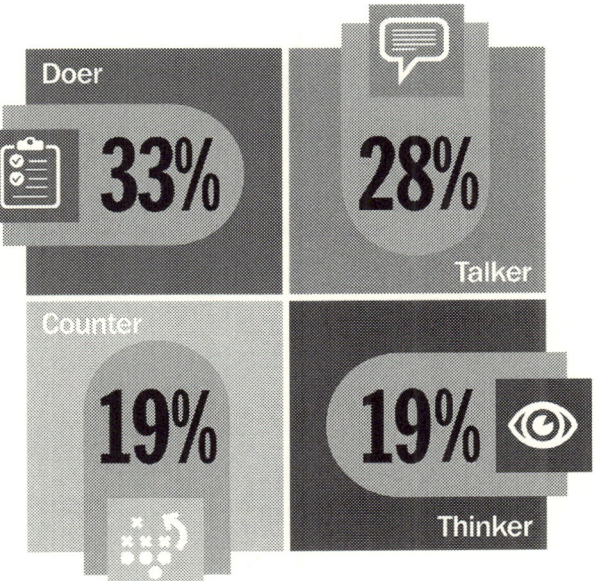

Grid Report Summary

It is important to understand that you are a very unique and exceptional combination of all the preferences and behaviors presented on this Career & Work-Life Grid; yet everyone leans more one way or the other. The areas of the Grid where you are the strongest are your predominant strengths and they will typically be those areas in which you most easily excel and develop skills. Your strengths are what motivate and create drive within you. Those other areas, where you are not as strong, are not necessarily a weakness, but they may represent a bias on your part that can limit what you ultimately achieve. Think of the Grid as a series of filters through which you view your world. The value of this improved self-knowledge is the ability to capitalize on your strengths without letting your biases stand in your way.

© Team Excellence, Inc. All rights reserved.

Page 1

(Cheryl Bergen's Career & Work-Life Grid)

Another benefit of the Team Excellence approach to psychometric assessment lay in the "At-A-Glance"-style Team Strengths Inventory reports. In just minutes, she could assess and compare each member of senior management's orientation toward tasks, relationships, thinking and procedures, as well as his behavioral and performance strengths when it came to working with others, dealing with change, preferred pace, identity, asserting himself, expressing his feelings, and his typical attention to detail.

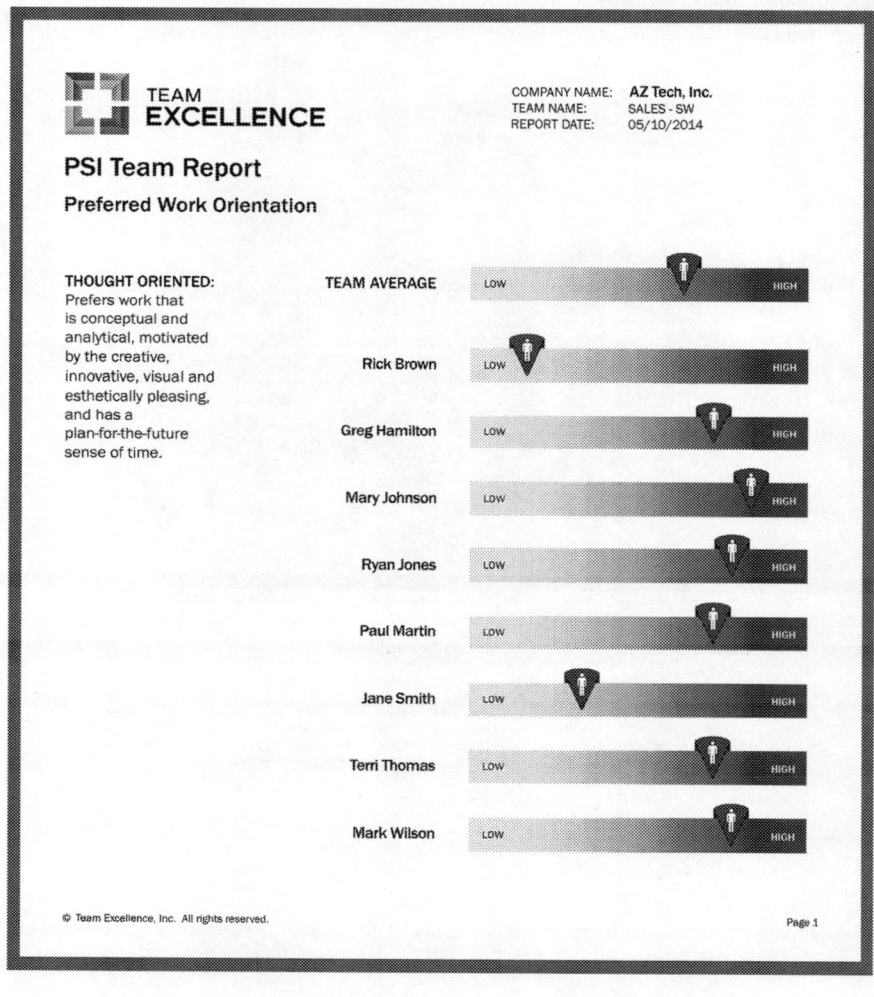

(Sample Team Report on Thought Orientation)

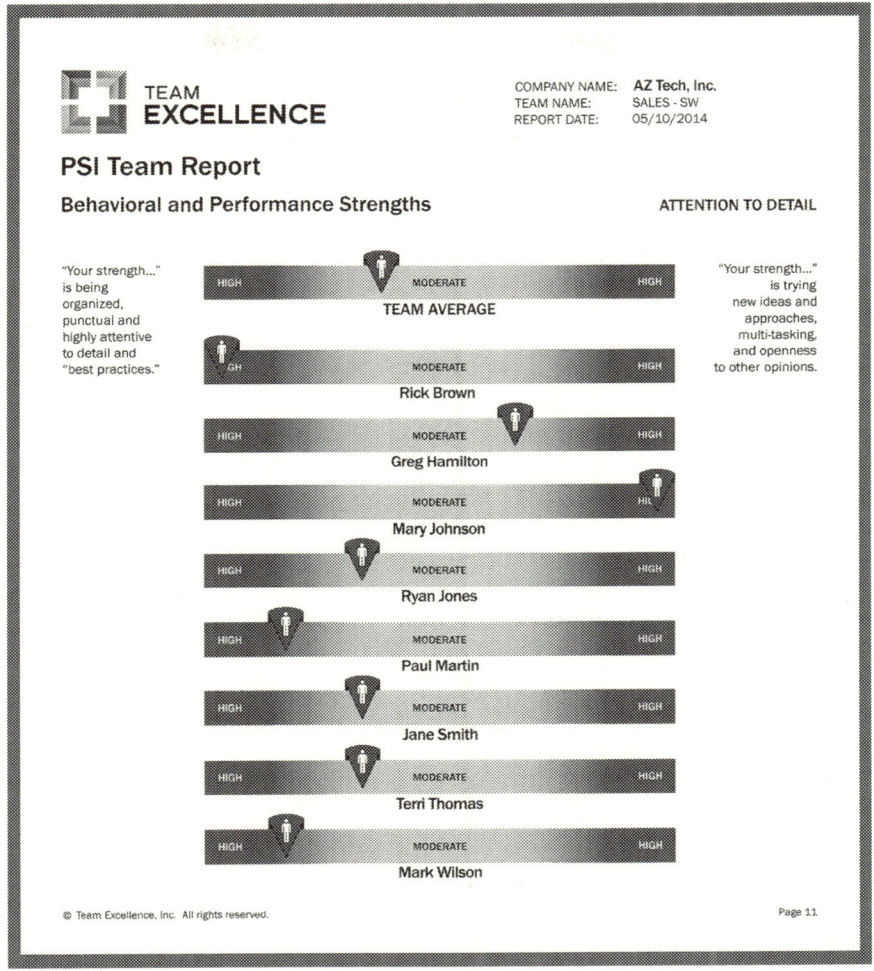

© Team Excellence, Inc. All rights reserved.

(Sample Team Report on Attention to Detail)

Based on the Team Strengths Inventory as well as PSI reports of every senior manager, Cheryl saw that AZ-Tech management was well balanced. She also inferred how every manager influenced the company culture and his "silo" within the culture. For example, Cheryl recognized what she'd always known about Colin—that he was the antithesis of the "old-school management" style. As a Thinker (purple) and a Talker (green), he possessed not just a strong philosophic belief and commitment to innovative ideas, but a strong commitment to the welfare of his employees. He was a "people's CEO." He wanted to put employees "first," and build a business culture that stood above the traditional organization. Hence, his quick "buy in" to the TDS.

However, his purple/green split also meant that he was often torn between bottom-line financial necessity and the desire to make people-pleasing decisions. He struggled over finding the right balance, and felt guilty when he had to sacrifice what he considered his staff's interests and expectations. He tried to find ways of "making up" for any decisions that disappointed his employees.

Senior VP of Operations Frank Girardi was also keen to please Colin and his own staff. However, Frank's PSI revealed a different mind-set and preferences—one more typical of "old school" leaders. Yet Frank was a guy who said what he meant and meant what he said. He was someone you could rely on to get the job done—on-time, on-spec and above-and-beyond expectations.

Whereas Colin was representative of the new breed of "servant leaders," understanding his role as one of "pointing employees to the future" by providing resources, support, and top-down empowerment to employees, Frank was all about issuing orders to the troops and monitoring their compliance with a thinly gloved iron fist. Although Frank did care about people, he was usually so focused on immediate, tangible results and on doing things the "right way" (his way), that he usually came across as an inflexible autocrat and bean counter. In fact, his nickname—*never* to be spoken in his presence—was "Kaiser Frank & Beans."

As in most organizations, managers serve as the "foot soldiers" of good leaders, focusing more on the tactical implementation of systems, policies, and the daily work performance of employees. But Kelly Anderson and Gary Monroe were far more than just foot soldiers. Instead, they were like Stonewall Jackson to Colin's Robert E. Lee. They both were brilliant strategists and gifted tacticians.

Before coming to AZ-Tech, Kelly had been the protégé of a highly respected marketing guru and played a major role in some very successful rebranding efforts. She was innovative, interpersonally sensitive and aware, and displayed a good balance between empathy for her employees and pragmatic bottom-line results. This was not surprising since Kelly "lived" mostly in the Talker (green) and Thinker (purple) quadrants. She had a major stake in the ground branding AZ-Tech's identity and product line in an effort to significantly increase its market share and to grow through acquisitions. Unfortunately, the focus on rapid growth through acquisitions had produced (as noted earlier) some unforeseen and negative consequences.

Gary Monroe was a Thinker (purple) and an enlightened Doer (blue). He knew everything about developing and building new products, but almost nothing about managing people. Fortunately, he knew that he lacked people skills and was open to improvement, especially since he had a strong distaste for "old school" behavior. The TDS and its TC contract made all the sense in the world to him, and he was embracing them with energy and enthusiasm. In some respects, Gary needed to borrow a chapter from Frank and become a stronger Doer about managing his people, especially when it came to reigning in their unbridled freewheeling enthusiasm. A department filled with free-thinking Einsteins might be "fun" in theory, but in reality it produced barely controlled chaos because he often lacked the discipline to lead his "troops" into a cohesive unit that was focused on achieving *near-term* goals—that could be touched, felt, and SOLD to the consumer in time to beat their competitors.

Cheryl laughed to herself. *If I were Dr. Frankenstein, I'd combine the strengths of every team member into a single super-leader. Then I'd clone them, and market the lot for ten million bucks apiece. Heck. Ten million would be a bargain.*

Chapter 6
ORGANIZATIONS HOLD EMPLOYEES ACCOUNTABLE

PARS: PERFORMANCE ASSESSMENT & REVIEW SYSTEM

In Chapter 1, we discussed the dramatic changes occurring in the economy, including evolving expectations about jobs and careers on the part of the *emerging workforce*. One of the most significant changes in these expectations is that of frequent, if not continuous, personal feedback on work performance. In this age of instant communication, employees want and need to receive much more feedback than organizations and managers were previously expected (or trained) to provide. Employees are constantly asking (at least on a subconscious level), "How am I doing?"

This expectation collides with the current habits and processes of meaningful performance feedback—something that can be inordinately costly for the unprepared organization. More than ever before, employees need measurable scoreboards. They need to know where they stand and how they are doing. Organizations that do not understand this, or choose to do nothing about it, will not be able to employ or retain the best employees. The competitive disadvantage of this error in leadership judgment is significant—maybe even life-threatening to the organization.

Consider the results of the following surveys published by *The New York Times* in May 2010:

> The Conference Board reported recently that just 45 percent of workers are satisfied with their jobs, down from 61 percent in 1987. The findings, based on a survey of 5,000 households, show that the decline goes well beyond concerns about job security. Employees are unhappy about the design of their jobs, the health of their organizations and the quality of their managers.
>
> A number of studies have documented the health toll of workplace stress, showing that unhappy workers are at higher risk for heart problems and depression, among other things...
>
> Samuel A. Culbert, a clinical psychologist who teaches at the Anderson School of Management at the University of California, Los Angeles, says too many people work in a "toxic" environment, and the title of his new book (from Hachette) throws a spotlight on one of the culprits: *Get Rid of the Performance Review!*
>
> Annual reviews not only create a high level of stress for workers, he argues, but end up making everybody— bosses and subordinates—less effective at their jobs. He says reviews are so subjective—so dependent on the worker's relationship with the boss—as to be meaningless. He says he has heard from countless workers who say their work life was ruined by an unfair review. "There is a very bad set of values that are embedded in the air because of performance reviews," he said.

We agree with the problem, but we take a different tack toward the solution.

We developed PARS, the *Performance Assessment & Review System*, with these types of development and personnel management issues in mind. PARS is more than state-of-the-art, Web-based performance appraisal software. It's *much* more than that.

Why is PARS different from annual performance appraisal systems— besides the fact that it can or should be administered more than once a year?

- PARS uses a proprietary values-based model for assessment—for getting the job done and getting it done right.

- The model that PARS uses is compatible and complementary to the PSI model, so it facilitates learning and integrating the TDS system.

- PARS is customizable to the client's needs, employee base, job definitions, and competencies, though most clients choose to use our recommended and proven competencies.

- PARS software is very flexible in its variety of assessment assignments—e.g., manager only, manager and employee, full 360s, etc., and can administer any combination or permutation simultaneously. Many companies need more than one system to accomplish this and do not have the benefit of an integrated database for ongoing historic review and gap analysis.

- PARS is more than just an online software product to be used periodically, however, often, the client chooses that to be. It's a business process woven into the Team Development Strategy that drives ongoing and routine dialogue/conversation (daily, weekly, monthly, quarterly, etc.) between a manager and an employee. It focuses on Team Covenant accountability for continuous performance improvement, coached specifically for that improvement, and provides frequent feedback to bring about and sustain growth and improvement. The reviews themselves won't get the job done, but currently, most organizations don't even have the right models and behaviors in place.

- PARS, in tandem with PSI, builds the foundation necessary to establish, nurture, and sustain *trust*.

PARS software can accommodate the straightforward needs of smaller organizations and the more complex needs of larger organizations as well. For small companies, PARS offers a simple-to-administer, turn-on-a-dime performance appraisal solution for a small staff with a flat-line management structure. For large organizations, PARS provides multidivisional, multidepartmental performance appraisal that allows for various levels of controlled managerial access—for data entry, appraisal administration, and report retrieval purposes.

Clients have total control over the creation and deployment of assessment criteria and can choose to utilize a variety of question and survey response types for both standard job classification assessment competencies and specific personalized job performance goals for each individual. Clients also determine *who* evaluates *whom* and *what* and can limit the access of certain confidential performance competencies to the individual employee and his manager, while allowing others to assess more general designated performance competencies.

The system is a very straightforward and intuitive online process that provides every employee with confidential access to individualized user accounts. Automated tracking and management of each employee's participation throughout a designated survey period includes a series of automated e-mail reminders about the individual's incomplete assignments throughout that survey period. Authorized client administrators and designated managers also have continuous online access to real-time status reports.

PARS represents the best of thirty-plus years of performance assessment expertise in organizations of all sizes and provides what our clients consistently report as the best, fastest, least intrusive and easiest to use appraisal process they've ever experienced.

Performance appraisal no longer has to be an annual event that must be completed to satisfy a bureaucratic requirement from the human resource department. It's not a process that has to bring the entire organization to a standstill while it conducts the annual "let's get it over with" ritual. PARS makes performance assessment quick and easy, allowing job-related feedback to become what it's supposed to be—an ongoing conversation between employees and managers that's designed to raise performance.

Again, one of the reasons for creating PARS was that we could not find any existing software program that accomplished everything we wanted to do. One of the most important missing functions was the ability to effectively deal with the Team Covenant and differentiate between measuring performance competencies and the demonstration of values.

We wanted an appraisal process that could distinguish between *getting the job done* and *getting it done right,* and we wanted to visually show these differences. It was important to connect the dots between performance assessment, our personality assessment and our organizational assessment methods. This will become easier to understand once you learn about all three of our assessment tools.

The PARS model combines assessment of job-related performance with relational-based behavior and segregates the two in order to objectively and quantitatively evaluate Team Covenant accountabilities.

Performance competencies evaluate the achievement of tasks, knowledge, and skills that have been identified as necessary for acceptable job performance. We evaluate the values side of the model based on the observations of interpersonal behavior prescribed by the Team Covenant. We refer to these competencies as "Demonstrated Values," since we are not clinically assessing values—only observing behavior.

Using an X-Y grid, which is visually similar and conceptually complementary to the PSI model, PARS presents its visual summary of the entire assessment report. By using these two complementary models, performance appraisal is directly associated with personality assessment.

The following illustration of the PARS Model is based on the administration of a full 360° performance assessment, meaning the appraisal survey was addressed by the individual, her immediate manager, and a representative group of colleagues and peers. For a manager, colleagues would typically be a group of their direct reports. For non-management employees, the colleagues would typically be a group of teammates or other workers who interact with the employee on a regular basis.

In the PARS system, this Summary Grid calculates Performance Competency responses against the horizontal axis. It calculates Demonstrated Values responses against the vertical axis.

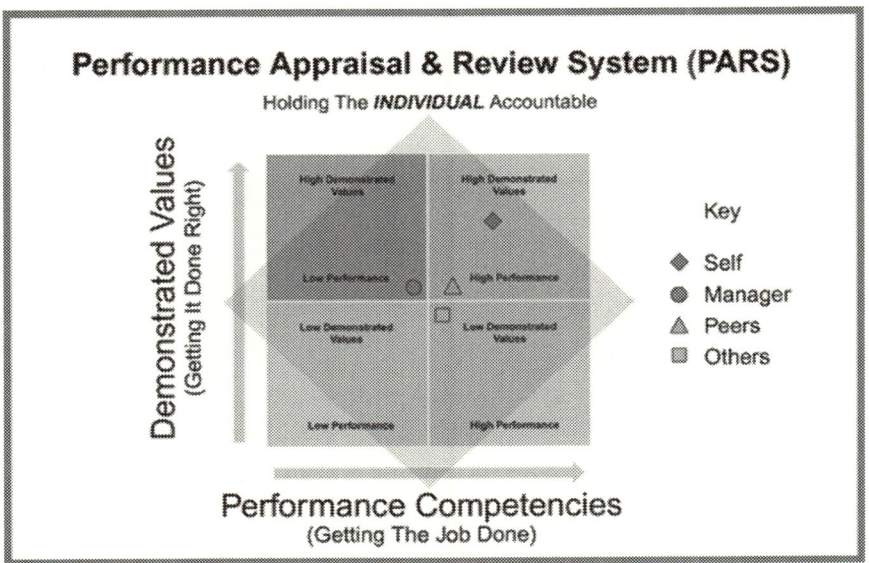

(PARS Performance Summary Grid Model)

This Summary Grid is an effective visual picture of the entire PARS assessment report, and is presented at the beginning of the report as a quick reference and overview. The report then proceeds to an item-by-item presentation of total responses to the survey, including suggestions for improvement of performance by the respondents.

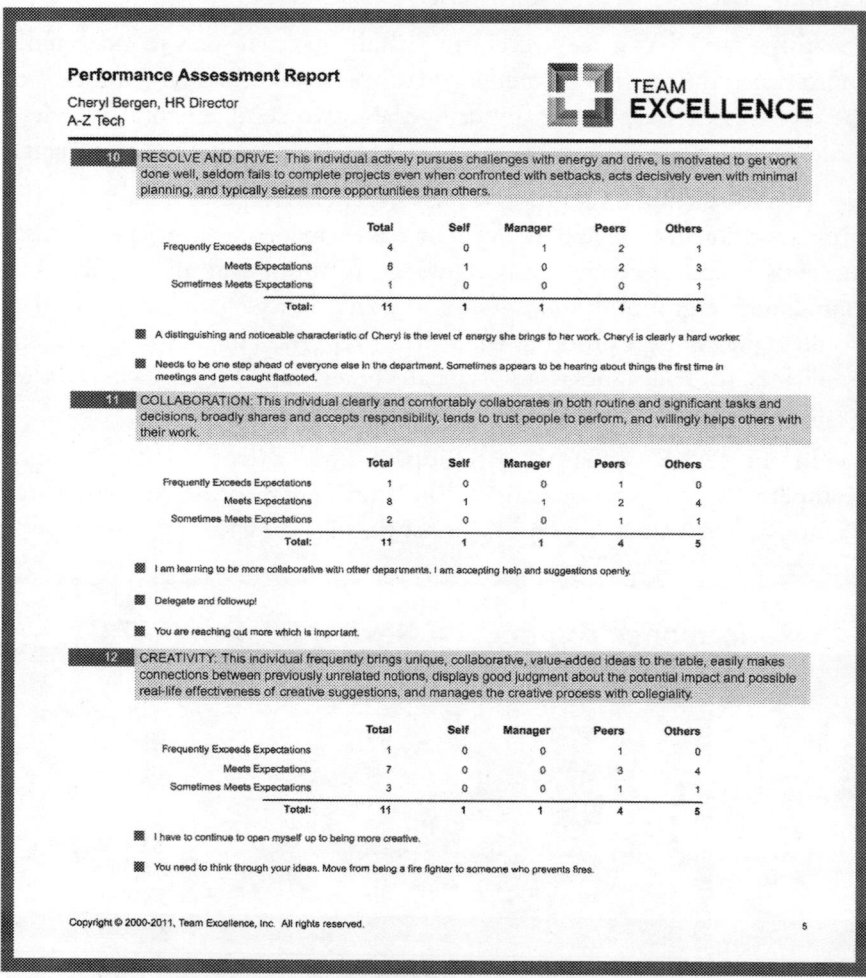

Performance Assessment Report

Cheryl Bergen, HR Director
A-Z Tech

TEAM EXCELLENCE

10 RESOLVE AND DRIVE: This individual actively pursues challenges with energy and drive, is motivated to get work done well, seldom fails to complete projects even when confronted with setbacks, acts decisively even with minimal planning, and typically seizes more opportunities than others.

	Total	Self	Manager	Peers	Others
Frequently Exceeds Expectations	4	0	1	2	1
Meets Expectations	6	1	0	2	3
Sometimes Meets Expectations	1	0	0	0	1
Total:	**11**	**1**	**1**	**4**	**5**

▨ A distinguishing and noticeable characteristic of Cheryl is the level of energy she brings to her work. Cheryl is clearly a hard worker.

▨ Needs to be one step ahead of everyone else in the department. Sometimes appears to be hearing about things the first time in meetings and gets caught flatfooted.

11 COLLABORATION: This individual clearly and comfortably collaborates in both routine and significant tasks and decisions, broadly shares and accepts responsibility, tends to trust people to perform, and willingly helps others with their work.

	Total	Self	Manager	Peers	Others
Frequently Exceeds Expectations	1	0	0	1	0
Meets Expectations	8	1	1	2	4
Sometimes Meets Expectations	2	0	0	1	1
Total:	**11**	**1**	**1**	**4**	**5**

▨ I am learning to be more collaborative with other departments. I am accepting help and suggestions openly.

▨ Delegate and followup!

▨ You are reaching out more which is important.

12 CREATIVITY: This individual frequently brings unique, collaborative, value-added ideas to the table, easily makes connections between previously unrelated notions, displays good judgment about the potential impact and possible real-life effectiveness of creative suggestions, and manages the creative process with collegiality.

	Total	Self	Manager	Peers	Others
Frequently Exceeds Expectations	1	0	0	1	0
Meets Expectations	7	0	0	3	4
Sometimes Meets Expectations	3	0	0	1	1
Total:	**11**	**1**	**1**	**4**	**5**

▨ I have to continue to open myself up to being more creative.

▨ You need to think through your ideas. Move from being a fire fighter to someone who prevents fires.

Copyright © 2000-2011, Team Excellence, Inc. All rights reserved.

5

(Sample PARS Survey Individual Items Report)

DON'T CHOKE THE HORSE

Historically, one of the biggest problems with performance appraisal has been that organizations try to do too much, too fast. Time and time again, companies give managers and employees fifteen, twenty, or more performance improvement goals in a single review cycle. Time and time again, I've witnessed virtually no improvement in performance as a result. What has your experience been?

I've believed for a long time that it's far better to assign just a few goals to a manager or employee, maybe three or four, but to make sure these are *truly* the most important goals—ones that, if achieved, will make the greatest impact on the person's overall performance. Once those goals are reached, the individual can be given several more. My experience with this approach is it works, and it works consistently.

With one of the forerunners of what is today PARS, a client tried to do far too much. The company was attempting to "kill a couple of birds" with one stone, and also wanted to use performance appraisal to document its compliance with a federal regulatory program. The result was that some employees had as many as fifty individual performance goals to be evaluated. The process ground to a halt. What was to have taken a couple of weeks dragged on for months. In addition, there was absolutely no measurable improvement in employee performance.

The client's overall result was that nothing positive happened. The system left such a bad taste in everyone's mouth that a couple of years passed before the organization sought out a proactive performance appraisal approach again. Now, this client limits its Performance Competencies to no more than eight and the same number for the Demonstrated Values it evaluates.

By taking this streamlined approach to performance appraisal, our most successful clients use PARS in the way it was intended. The highest priorities get addressed, and the most important performance improvements are achieved. As important as anything else, people now *accept* the system. They look forward to using it because it produces fair and measurable results without being an overwhelming, time-consuming burden. Performance appraisal facilitates work, rather than impede it. So as we say in Texas, "Don't choke the horse!"

Today, there may be no more important responsibility for managers than being effective coaches and mentors. Many managers are promoted to their positions because they were extremely successful at doing a job. An assumption was made that they would be good at getting others to do that same job. Unfortunately, this is not always true. As stated earlier, many managers are "superdoers" and never become effective at leading others.

Earlier, we talked about management belief systems and tried to confront the problem of old-school managers who think they must use power and control to get people to accomplish their tasks. The Team Covenant promotes a management philosophy and belief under which people will willingly take ownership of work, and approach their jobs from what we've called the "intrepreneurial" attitude of responsibility.

PERFORMANCE COACHING
AND MENTORING

One key element driving the success of this process is the coaching and mentoring clients provide to their employees. It's a vital component, given the changing expectations of employees today and their ongoing need for instant feedback.

A traditional drawback to coaching and mentoring, however, has been a lack of specific, objective information on how the individual is doing his job—current information. Without this, coaching is like trying to improve an athlete's performance based on repeating the rules of the game, rather than offering specific examples of what the individual is doing well and not doing as well. The results of coaching significantly improve when current and ongoing feedback is provided, particularly when the feedback is based on narrowly defined goals that the individual accepts responsibility for achieving. Our clients successfully use PARS to both establish and document the "yardstick" needed to make coaching specific and meaningful.

Again, the analogy of a scoreboard is apt. Consider what the experience and outcome of a game would be without constant feedback from a real-time scoreboard.

What would you expect the final results of a basketball or football game to be if they were played without a scoreboard? Obviously, they'd be confusing at best and probably chaotic. The final score would surely be subject to argument and debate.

To complete the analogy, now consider how the total season would progress without an ability to coach an individual or team on what's working and not working. Development and improvement of performance over the course of a season would be significantly handicapped.

Effective coaching and mentoring requires accurate and continuous data streams, not just the general impressions that managers and supervisors typically offer—impressions that are often more subjective than objective.

PARS was designed to be much more than simply an annual performance appraisal system to satisfy the organizational ritual of once-a-year reviews. The system was intended to be easier to administer, track, and deliver than more conventional systems—one that can deliver more frequent cycles of results, if desired. It was also intended to encompass more than just measuring the results of the job. It was designed to assess a values-based approach and confirm that the individual is getting the job done *correctly*, according to Team Covenant standards. Our clients tell us that PARS is meeting all of these expectations, and in doing so, providing fair and objective performance feedback that's ideally suited to effective, ongoing coaching and mentoring.

CONTINUOUS IMPROVEMENT

Another shortcoming of the traditional annual review process is the assumption that improving performance is something to be addressed once a year. Most organizations pay perfunctory attention, at best, to performance improvement except when the annual review cycle approaches. To invoke our sports analogy again, no baseball team would ever get to the World Series if everyone ignored their performance until the end of the regular season.

An integral part of our Team Development Strategy addressed within the Team Covenant is the obligation of all managers and employees to engage in continuous performance improvement. Without a strong focus on and an acceptance of this obligation, improving performance is usually tied to receiving an increase in compensation and not to everyone's *intrepreneurial* responsibility.

For organizations to be as competitive as possible, it's essential that they build this business-strategy commitment to *never* being satisfied with current results. Companies must create a cultural expectation that performance can and must be improved. This commitment becomes a major competitive advantage for our clients—one that's an integral component of their total business strategy.

BUILDING THE RIGHT PERFORMANCE COMPETENCIES

As with most things in life, there are several good approaches to creating performance appraisal surveys. If your goal is to use annual assessment reviews as a way to document—in great detail—what employees accomplish (using reviews for the purpose of historical record keeping), then it's appropriate to use lengthy surveys. On the other hand, if your goal is to use performance appraisal as a tool for driving continuous improvement and then measuring that improvement, you'll want a different approach. Competencies are the possession of knowledge, skills, experience, and desire. The key to measuring competencies is to properly define them. We are not talking about *competencies* versus *values*; we are talking about them in this way:

- *Performance Competencies* define traditional job performance requirements of knowing what to do—how to do the professional or technical functions and activities associated with an assigned job, based on knowledge, disciplines (accounting, engineering, administrative, leadership, etc.), and demonstrated accomplishments.

- *Values Competencies* define the relational or interpersonal skills and performance requirements of honoring the Team Covenant. In PARS, we call them "Demonstrated Values," because PARS is not a clinical assessment of what values you *believe*. Instead, PARS reflects observations of the interpersonal behavior you demonstrate in the performance of your job. The Team Covenant stipulates, among other things, that the organization is a customer-driven organization (internally and externally) and that every employee is also a customer. That takes some paradigm shifting for some.

We developed the PARS software to function with great flexibility. It can be used in a variety of ways, using different assessment models and with a virtually unlimited number of survey competencies and questions. Again, we lean strongly toward brief surveys. Performance assessment that's based on a few high-priority, easy-to-measure expectations is more likely to produce *achievable* results and create a work environment capable of sustaining a business system (your system) of continuous improvement.

Experience suggests that focusing a manager's and employee's attention on accomplishing several "most important" performance improvement goals will consistently produce better results than trying to get an individual to "fix" a dozen or more things all at once. So we always approach continuous improvement as a work in progress and encourage our clients to think of employee development as an ongoing, never-ending process. This approach supports the implementation of the Team Covenant which becomes an integral part of the organization's culture and behavior.

Now, let's tackle the choice and development of the right performance competencies. If you choose to take a more traditional approach to performance review and only want to assess the tactical or technical aspects of doing the job, you will only want to define those job-related criteria that we classify as *performance competencies.*

However, if you are ready to embrace the Team Development Strategy as an organization-wide business system and culture, then you are prepared to use the Team Covenant as the definition of your philosophy and leadership commitment. With this, you will want to develop both *performance competencies* and *demonstrated values competencies.*

Again, the performance competencies will measure the knowledge, skills, experience, and desire your managers and employees are expected to have to do their jobs effectively. The demonstrated values will define the individual and interpersonal behaviors for which your employees will be held accountable to get the work done in accordance with Team Covenant. An easy way to remember the difference is that performance competencies measure *getting the job done,* while demonstrated values competencies measure *getting it done right.*

You may want to develop different sets of performance competencies if your organization has a lot of job classifications, and the basic requirements for each classification are unique. But don't assume you must do this. Some of the most complex client organizations still "keep it simple" by having only a handful of performance competencies: one for nonmanagement roles, one for middle-management roles, and one for senior management roles. They save the task of measuring specific job assignments and/or goals for the Individual Goals component of PARS, which will be discussed later.

Performance competencies can be most effective when they are general enough to define the expectations for almost everyone, especially when those expectations are directly related to the obligations required by the Team Covenant. Managers are often expected to perform functionally in different ways than nonmanagers, and senior managers should be expected to tackle leadership functions that exceed the expectations of everyone else.

We strongly encourage using a limited number of performance competencies for each job classification of work you choose to define. Our most successful clients have only eight to ten performance competencies for every job classification. Please remember, don't choke the horse Developing and selecting the right competencies, both for performance and demonstrated values, is a critical factor, but don't insist on getting everything perfect from the get-go. PARS will be an evolution in your experiences, one you'll want to refine based on the responses and results you receive in your initial application. That said, it's also important to start a process that will bring consistency to your ongoing review cycles.

You will achieve the greatest results through PARS, by measuring a fairly consistent set of competencies year after year. Evaluating performance against a consistent yardstick produces the best results.

SETTING INDIVIDUAL GOALS

PARS is also programmed to let you assign each manager and employee individualized goals specifically designed for their personal performance. We believe this is the very best approach to developing continuous improvement. This is particularly true if the assignment of individual goals follows the same guidelines suggested for the other competencies.

Individual goals should be few in number and reflect the highest priorities for improvement in individual performance. The goals should be specific and when possible, they should also be quantifiable. To tell an employee that you want them to improve their verbal communications skills is not a very well-defined goal. It's much better to say that you want the person to successfully complete a course in public speaking during the first six months of the year. You can measure that goal and determine whether it was accomplished or not. Another example would be to tell a sales employee that you want her to close one new account each month during the year or that you want them to increase their sales volume by 15 percent during the year. That's a much more productive approach than merely saying you want them to increase sales.

Another consideration in assigning individual goals is setting clear and measurable goals at the very *beginning* of the year. If an employee is to be held accountable for achieving a yearlong objective, he should be given the entire year to accomplish it. Too often, employees learn what their annual goals are in the final months or even weeks of the review cycle. First, that isn't fair to the employee. Second, it never produces good results.

Individual goals assigned to employees are reported separately in their personal PARS reports. These goals are calculated on the horizontal axis, along with general performance competencies, so they can be included in the Performance Summary Grid.

Remember that employees are much more successful in achieving all of their goals when these goals are discussed and reviewed frequently. Don't make the mistake of waiting until December 1 to determine what progress has been made. Conduct a meeting at least once a month to discuss progress and, for some employees, weekly meetings may be more effective. If employees postpone or procrastinate in tackling goals, discourage this through the use of early and frequent reviews to measure results, and find out what additional help or resources they may need. In addition, encourage success by finding ways to bestow appropriate and sincere recognition for their short-term successes, whenever possible.

With individual goals especially, but with any performance expectation, it is important to confirm that the employee understands precisely what is expected. Do not merely ask people if they understand what to do.

Most will always say "yes," even if they're clueless. People rarely admit that they don't understand. They don't want to look stupid. A better approach is to ask the employee to tell you in her own words how she plans to achieve the assigned goal. That's the best time to verify that clear communication has occurred. It is so much better than finding out there was a misunderstanding just before the deadline. Used correctly, the individual goals section of PARS can be the most productive contributor to the whole process.

USING A 360° ASSESSMENT APPROACH

Traditional performance appraisal reviews are conducted by an employee's immediate manager or supervisor, and sometimes by the individual himself. Although this type of assessment is valuable and better than no review at all, it limits the perspective of how well the employee is doing since a manager can't be observing everything at all times.

This limitation is most significant when the organizational goal is to get employees to accept a personal sense of ownership for their work and buy in to an *intrepreneurial* attitude of accountability. When employees disagree with the evaluation of their manager, the intuitive rationale is that the "boss" just didn't see it all. It's a fair argument that a solo perspective is subjective and isn't a complete and objective view of the employee's overall performance.

Hence, there has been a growing acceptance of what is commonly referred to as 360° assessment (or just "360"). This assessment assembles the collective perspectives of the individual, his manager or managers, a representative group of his peers or colleagues, and a representative group of people who report directly to the individual... or who are influenced by his performance.

The argument for 360° assessments is that they produce a more objective report, especially when a consensus is reached. If one person believes a certain level of performance is occurring, *this* can be fairly considered a subjective observation. But when ten out of twelve respondents agree on a particular level of performance, this is a much more reliable (and certainly a more objective) point of view.

The 360° assessment process has been widely used for management staff. It is fairly common for managers to have their performance evaluated by their supervisors, their peers, and their subordinates. What is *not* yet typical in most organizations is the use of the 360° approach for the entire workforce.

Since one of the stipulations of the Team Covenant is that all employees share a genuine sense of ownership for their portion of the organization's total success, it's logical for employees to hold one another accountable for their performances and use 360° performance evaluations to achieve a more objective result. This is already being done successfully with a growing number of clients. I don't want to suggest that this is an instant solution. It's not.

The successful use of 360° evaluations will reflect an evolution within the organization. Getting employees to accept the responsibility of candidly evaluating their immediate supervisor is a big leap for a lot of organizations. And having employees evaluate one another can be an even larger leap. To achieve reliable results requires time—to develop a sufficient amount of trust and credibility in the organization's commitment to the Team Covenant.

We suggest that clients take incremental steps in moving toward the use of 360° evaluations throughout their organizations. We recommend that clients begin with the use of 360° performance appraisals for their senior management team, and use the more conventional manager-over-employee review process for everyone else. Over a period of time, the organization can gradually include additional levels of managers and employees in the 360° process.

PARS is uniquely designed to allow this combination of performance appraisal processes to be deployed simultaneously. Organizations are best served by taking a *graduated* approach to administering 360° performance appraisals to all employee levels. To expect every employee within an organization to participate objectively and correctly in a 360° assessment process stretches the initial capabilities of most companies. Without proper training, the process can become very political and result in popularity contests. So it is very important to let the 360° process evolve gradually, as everyone in the organization comes to understand the value and importance of employees accepting individual responsibility and accountability for the organization's success.

WHO DOES THE EVALUATING?

If PARS is used as a traditional evaluation process, where the manager is the only person reviewing the employee's performance, this is a no-brainer. The PARS software is programmed to make this designation easily. With just a simple check of a box in the survey assignment process, individual surveys will be ready for use during the next review cycle. If, however, the performance evaluations are to include others, whether a full-blown 360° assessment or a hybrid 360° format, PARS still makes the designations easy with the same check of a box in the survey assignment process. Again, all of the individual surveys will be appropriately populated and ready for deployment during the next review cycle.

PARS is organized so that each employee's record is grouped within the department in which the employee works. During the process of assigning assessment relationships, it's easy to select who will evaluate each employee and what his assigned relationship will be, using simple, intuitive menus that list all the employees in that department. Reviewers are also offered a choice of assessment relationships by checking boxes that designate which survey items each respondent will be presented during the evaluation. Simple editing options are available when employee evaluations require cross-department assignments.

The entire review process is automated. Every employee has access to a discrete personal login account, where all assigned reviews are made available. The reviews do not require decisions or survey management selections by the employee.

SELECTING THE RATING SCALE

PARS provides several rating scales from which the organization's administrator can select. These scales include true-false, yes-no, open-ended comment questions, and multiple-point or Likert scale ratings. Some competencies or questions lend themselves to a true-false or yes-no response. Often, individual goals and goals that are specific and quantified are best handled this way. If a goal is to accomplish a specific quantity of something, or a specific percentage, then it either happened or it did not.

Since the knowledge of whether these specific goals is usually limited to the individual employee and her manager, true-false and yes-no questions are best used for this relationship. Other managers, peers, and employees will probably not know with certainty whether these quantifiable goals have been accomplished, and sometimes goals that are this specific may be confidential.

Because we believe in brevity and focusing on high-priority performance improvements, we do not recommend using a lot of open-ended comment questions. There may be situations or circumstances that require the use of these questions, but in our experience, these situations will be rare. The most common use of open-ended questions is at the end of the survey, when you need to ask if there's anything the respondent believes important for the performance improvement of the individual under evaluation— something that wasn't previously asked or addressed.

Most people are familiar with multiple-point scales that rate opinions and judgments from an extremely desirable to extremely undesirable. The scale is named after a prominent American psychologist, Rensis Likert.

We recommend the use of five-point Likert scale ratings for most of the evaluation competencies in demonstrated values, performance, and individual goals. Most competency statements are best stated in descriptions suited for the Likert scale, and it's this rating scale that drives calculation of the Performance Summary Grid. This grid is a significant visual summary of the employee's overall performance and contributes in a variety of ways to effective coaching and mentoring.

Whether true-false, yes-no, open-ended, or Likert scale ratings selections, PARS offers great flexibility in the application and combination of these scales. It produces an easy-to-administer-and-understand survey, as well as a user-friendly array of report formats.

IMPLEMENTING PARS AT AZ-TECH

To initiate the implementation of PARS, Cheryl Bergen followed a procedure similar to the one she'd used to launch the PSI system. She developed a timeframe to roll out the process over the next six months, set up the company's discrete and confidential online PARS account, and designated herself as the administrator. From there, she provided Team Excellence with all the employee data needed to create an AZ-Tech PARS database, and then started PARS training and support for department heads and team leaders Using guidelines and templates provided by Team Excellence, Cheryl and her HR Staff also:

1. Determined department assignments to be used in PARS assessments.

2. Determined organization-wide values competencies for the PARS assessments.

3. Determined appropriate evaluation categories to be used in PARS assessments.

4. Determined appropriate performance competencies for evaluation categories.

5. Determined organizational policy for establishing and assigning individualized performance goals for all employees and managers.

6. Determined additional PARS assessment variables—e.g., rating scales and assessment perspective levels.

7. Determined PARS roll-out steps, timetable, and schedule.

8. Sent organizational-wide announcements about PARS implementation, reminding managers and employees about individual accountabilities and outlining the roll-out steps.

9. Conducted many PARS training sessions.

10. Scheduled the first PARS evaluation cycle and created individual employee and manager assessment assignments.

11. Launched the first PARS evaluation cycle.

12. Used the first PARS deployment to establish evaluation guidelines and follow-up procedures between employees and managers.

13. Helped establish AZ-Tech's Team Covenant commitments and her expectations on how to integrate PSI and PARS into future communications and coaching.

14. Determined schedules and intervals for ongoing deployment of PARS and distributed that information throughout the entire company.

15. Met with managers to determine their overall response to the initial PARS evaluations, with a focus on the continued use of PARS reports to help managers coach employees and determine managers' additional training needs.

16. Conducted small group discussions with employees as a follow-up to the initial PARS evaluation and solicited feedback on understanding, opportunities to use PARS and PSI feedback in daily work, as well as determining further training needs for employees in the use of PARS and PSI.

17. Developed a structure and timeframe for conducting ongoing training reinforcement for the TDS, as needed.

When it came to selecting evaluation categories and performance competencies for various managers and employees, Cheryl consulted with both managers and employees to set the yardsticks. For example, she discussed leadership performance competencies at a meeting of senior managers and later with each individual manager.

The initial results are on the following pages.

PARS Nonmanagement Performance Competencies

1. QUALITY OF WORK: Plans, organizes, and completes his/her work in a thorough, efficient, and accurate manner.

2. DEPENDABILITY: Accomplishes the duties of his/her position in a timely manner with little follow-up required. He/she reports to work on time and is seldom absent.

3. QUANTITY OF WORK: Maintains a high level of productivity and consistent work output.

4. RELEVANT JOB KNOWLEDGE/SKILLS: Understands his/her job requirements and demonstrates the necessary knowledge and skills to perform assigned tasks.

5. DECISION MAKING/PROBLEM SOLVING: Demonstrates the ability to recognize and solve problems and makes decisions in accordance with department and company standards.

6. SELF-MANAGEMENT: Demonstrates the ability to complete assignments successfully, taking responsibility for monitoring and reporting process, progress and results.

7. CUSTOMER SERVICE: Demonstrates a business commitment, a sense of urgency, and profit-motivation in meeting customer expectations.

8. CONTINUOUS IMPROVEMENT: Is willing to learn new skills, concepts and technology to become more efficient and productive in his/her job performance.

PARS Middle-Management Performance Competencies

1. ACTION ORIENTED: Enjoys working hard; is action oriented and full of energy for the things he/she sees as challenging; not fearful of acting with a minimum of planning; and seizes more opportunities than others.

2. COLLABORATION: Clearly and comfortably collaborates in both routine and important tasks and decisions; broadly shares both responsibility and accountability; tends to trust people to perform; and willing to help fellow employees with their own work.

3. DECISION MAKING: Makes decisions in a timely manner, sometimes with incomplete information and under tight deadlines and pressure; and able to make a quick decision.

4. ORGANIZING: Can marshal resources (people, ideas, material, support, and other resources) to get things done; can orchestrate multiple activities at once to accomplish a goal; uses resources effectively and efficiently; and arranges information and files in a useful manner.

5. PERSEVERANCE AND DRIVE: Pursues everything with energy, drive, and a need to finish; seldom gives up before finishing, especially in the face of resistance or setbacks; and is motivated to get work done well.

6. PRIORITY SETTING: Spends his/her time and the time of others on what's important; quickly zeros in on the critical few and puts the trivial many aside; can quickly sense what will help or hinder accomplishing a goal; eliminates roadblocks; and creates focus.

7. PROBLEM SOLVING: Uses rigorous logic and methods to solve difficult problems with effective solutions; probes all fruitful sources for answers; can see hidden problems; is excellent at honest analysis; and looks beyond the obvious and doesn't stop at the first answers.

8. TIME MANAGEMENT: Uses his/her time effectively and efficiently; values time; concentrates his/her efforts on the more important priorities; gets more done in less time than others; and can attend to a broader range of activities.

PARS Senior Leadership Performance Competencies

1. APPROACHABILITY: Is easy to approach and talk to; expends extra effort to put others at ease; can be warm, pleasant, and gracious; is sensitive to and patient with the interpersonal anxieties of others; builds rapport well; is a good listener; is an early knower, and getting informal and incomplete information in time to do something about it.

2. BUSINESS ACUMEN: Knows how businesses work; knowledgeable in current and possible future policies, practices, trends, developments in e-commerce and information affecting his/her business and organization; knows the competition; and is aware of how business strategies and tactics work in the marketplace.

3. COMMAND AND LEADERSHIP SKILLS: Relishes leading; takes unpopular stands if necessary; encourages direct and tough debate, but isn't afraid to end the debate and move on; is looked to for direction in a crisis; faces adversity head on; and energized by tough challenges

4. CREATIVITY: Comes up with a lot of new and unique ideas; easily makes connections among previously unrelated notions; and tends to be seen as original and value-added in brainstorming settings.

5. DECISION QUALITY: Makes good decisions (without considering how much time it takes) based on a mixture of analysis, wisdom, experience, and judgment; most of his/her solutions and suggestions are correct and accurate when judged over time; and sought out by others for advice and solutions.

6. HIRING AND STAFFING: Has a nose for talent; hires the best people available from the inside or outside; is not afraid of selecting strong people; and assembles talented staff.

7. LISTENING: Practices attentive and active listening; has the patience to hear people out; and can accurately restate the opinions of others even when he/she disagrees.

8. PROCESS MANAGEMENT: Good at figuring out the processes necessary to get things done; knows how to organize people and activities; understands how to separate and combine tasks into efficient workflow; knows what to measure and how to measure it; can see opportunities for synergy and integration where others can't; can simplify complex processes; and gets more out of fewer resources.

In addition, Cheryl solicited input from individuals and groups to determine the company-wide values competencies for the PARS assessments. They are detailed on the next page.

PARS Company-Wide Values Competencies

1. Treats others with dignity, respect and courtesy, and seldom loses his/her temper.

2. Recognizes the value of other's individuality and acknowledges the merit of other people's points of view.

3. Tries to do his/her best, strives for excellence, assumes accountability for the work he/she performs, and continuously attempts to grow and improve in the performance of his/her job.

4. Maintains a high level of honesty and integrity in the performance of his/her job.

5. Communicates clearly, professionally, and politely to management, fellow employees, investors, and others; expresses himself/herself in a courteous, mature and professional manner with everyone.

6. Demonstrates a high work ethic by being punctual, dependable, and conscientious, and has reliable attendance in the performance of his/her job.

7. In the event of a mistake, acknowledges the mistake, apologizes, and commits to trying harder and doing better.

8. Demonstrates a genuine commitment to and belief in the Team Covenant; uses the Covenant to guide his/her daily performance and behavior, and shares a sense of mutual ownership for successful organizational results through utilizing the Team Development Strategy.

All of the preceding competencies support A-Z Tech's corporate philosophy and are reflected its abbreviated Current-Year Business Plan Overview:

> AZ-TECH fulfills our mission, manages our staff, and accomplishes our business objectives through an innovative and nontraditional business plan process tied directly to our employee performance management system, the Team Development Strategy. This business plan process has established and assigned specific job-related goals for every manager and employee that are vertically integrated, by function and department, into supporting and achieving our total composite annual business plan.
>
> For the current budget year, the AZ-Tech business plan is to produce $1.3 billion in revenues, expend $1.1 billion in operating costs, and provide a gross contribution before taxes of $200 million.
>
> AZ-Tech's Chief Executive Officer assumes the specific and overall accountability for the achievement of these goals which have been approved by AZ-Tech's Board of Directors. The CEO's Executive Team and department managers assume individual accountability for achieving specifically designated, quantified, and clearly associated job-related goals in support of the CEO's ability to accomplish his responsibility. Every employee then assumes individual accountability for achieving specifically designated, quantified, and clearly associated

job-related goals in support of their manager's ability to accomplish his or her responsibility.

This bottom-to-top vertically integrated approach to business planning and performance management allows AZ-Tech to build measurable and individual accountability throughout our organization, respond flexibly to changing business requirements and market conditions that may occur throughout the budget year, and remain innovative in our commitment to the Team Development Strategy and sustaining a business culture focused on continuous growth and improvement on the part of every manager and employee.

Chapter 7
EMPLOYEES HOLD THE ORGANIZATION ACCOUNTABLE

In a story published by *The Atlantic Monthly* in January 2011, journalist Tim Kane wonders:

> Why are so many of the most talented officers now abandoning military life for the private sector? An exclusive survey of West Point graduates shows that it's not just money. Increasingly, the military is creating a command structure that rewards conformism and ignores merit. As a result, it's losing its vaunted ability to cultivate entrepreneurs in uniform.
>
> ...[T]he American military produce[s] the most innovative and entrepreneurial leaders in the country, then waste[s] that talent in a risk-averse bureaucracy.... Military leaders know they face a paradox. A widely circulated 2010 report from the Strategic Studies Institute of the Army War College said: "Since the late 1980s... prospects for the Officer Corps' future have been darkened by... plummeting company-grade officer retention rates. Significantly, this leakage includes a large share of high-performing officers." Similar alarms have been sounded for decades, starting long before the

wars in Iraq and Afghanistan made the exit rate of good officers an acute crisis When General Peter Schoomaker served as Army chief of staff from 2003 to 2007, he emphasized a "culture of innovation"... the Army did transform. But the talent crisis persisted for a simple reason: *the problem isn't cultural.* The military's problem is a deeply anti-entrepreneurial personnel structure. From officer evaluations to promotions to job assignments, all branches of the military operate more like a government bureaucracy with a unionized workforce than like a cutting-edge meritocracy.

It's convenient to believe that top officers simply have more lucrative opportunities in the private sector, and that their departures are inevitable. But the reason overwhelmingly cited by veterans and active-duty officers alike is that the military personnel system— every aspect of it—is nearly blind to merit. Performance evaluations emphasize a zero-defect mentality, meaning that risk-avoidance trickles down the chain of command. Promotions can be anticipated almost to the day— regardless of an officer's competence—so that there is essentially no difference in rank among officers the same age, even after 15 years of service. Job assignments are managed by a faceless, centralized bureaucracy that keeps everyone guessing where they might be shipped next.

In other words, says the author, the U.S. military—like many private sector organizations—is suffering from chronic *entitlement disease.* This is an attitude that states that all employees deserve rewards—benefits, vacation, holidays, recognition, and so forth—merely for showing up. In such organizations, there are few (if any) expectations built into the job to do more than the minimum. Worse, there's often little or no incentive for employees and managers to achieve their personal best and to help the organization succeed in its purpose and mission in a way that's consistent with the corporate culture and philosophy.

Any organization that expects employees to expend only enough skill and effort to achieve "passing grade" results will receive mediocre results in return—if that. Any organization that actually *rewards* staff for producing mediocre results by passing out the equivalent of "participation trophies" to anyone, and everyone is unwittingly creating a bureaucratic mind-set that discourages staff from trying to excel and further the company's goals.

Worse, the moment individual employees recognize that they cannot hold the company accountable for encouraging personal and team excellence, development and growth—for rewarding merit—most will adopt the "can't win/don't try" attitude of slacker champion Homer Simpson. From here, a cresting wave of futility will quickly engulf the entire business culture, discouraging innovation, free expression, and (eventually) organization-wide growth and profitability.

Enter PARS and the ESS (Employee Satisfaction Survey).

Managers should use PARS as one of the factors that influence their decisions about an employee's compensation adjustment. Managers need to learn to use good and encompassing judgment, rather than let one tool or set of data become a "crutch" and relieve them of their obligations to think and use good judgment. Using annual performance appraisal solely for the purpose of rationalizing compensation decisions is the main reason why traditional performance appraisal does not work. When compensation is the main purpose, performance appraisal systems become a political game in which managers don't do much to improve performance by coaching employees to develop and grow professionally. Instead, performance appraisals are used to justify decisions that were (typically) already made before the evaluation ever took place.

THE SYNERGY OF OUR
AWARD-WINNING SYSTEM

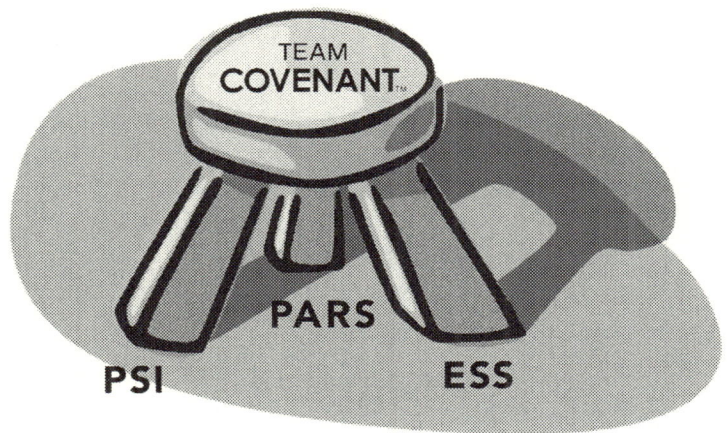

The Team Development Strategy is a three-legged stool. The platform is the Team Covenant, which is supported by three *equally* important legs:

- PSI is the tool that individuals use to hold themselves and fellow workers accountable—a way of looking in the mirror.

- PARS is the tool that the organization uses to hold employees accountable.

- ESS is the tool that employees use to hold the organization accountable.

EMPLOYEES DON'T EXPECT TO BE THE BOSS

Employees don't expect to be the boss. They don't expect to be in charge or get their way on every issue. What they *do* want is to have input—to have their ideas and opinions heard and their points of view respected. The Team Covenant promises the right of free expression without fear of negative consequences. This requires a genuine and sustained commitment from senior management to not just endorse this agreement but to *live it* and implement it constantly.

In Chapter 6, I referenced an article containing comments by Samuel Culbert, who believes that the traditional approach to performance reviews prohibits the kind of trusting relationships that make employee improvement possible. In a *New York Times* Op-Ed "Get Rid of the Performance Review!," Culbert lambasted the conventional performance review and suggested an alternative:

> Maybe your boss is all-knowing. But I've never seen one that was. In a self-interested world, where imperfect people are judging other imperfect people, anybody reviewing somebody else's performance—whether as an actor, a writer, a spouse, a friend or a worker—is subjective. It's why when employees switch bosses, more often than not their evaluation changes as well.
>
> Under such a system, in which one's livelihood can be destroyed by a self-serving boss trying to meet a budget

or please the higher-ups, what employee would ever speak his mind? What employee would ever say that the boss is wrong, and offer an idea on how something might get done better?

Only an employee looking for trouble.

Is there a way out? I believe there is, and it works for both government and business. It's something I call the *performance preview* [emphasis added]. Instead of top-down reviews, both boss and subordinate are held responsible for setting goals and achieving results. No longer will only the subordinate be held accountable for the often arbitrary metrics that the boss creates. Instead, bosses are taught how to truly manage, and learn that it's in their interest to listen to their subordinates to get the results the taxpayer is counting on.

Instead of the bosses merely handing out A's and C's, they work to make sure everyone can earn an A. And the word goes out: "No more after-the-fact disappointments. Tell me your problems as they happen; we're in it together and it's my job to ensure results."

Culbert's "preview" approach is akin to our Team Development Strategy—in setting goals on the front end, reviewing them and keeping them current.

Employees do expect and need to have a voice. They want to be heard and have their points of view respected. The ongoing communications process that evolves through the implementation of TDS, and the coaching process we recommend—where employees are given a bottom-up responsibility for using the reports generated by PARS and developing a self-determined improvement plan, taking that plan to their manager, and then discussing and negotiating the formal improvement plan—places the accountability for entrepreneurial ownership and continuous performance improvement *squarely on the individual employee*. Again, this is part of the Team Covenant and considerably different than the traditional approach disdained by Culbert.

ESS: AN ANNUAL
ORGANIZATION-WIDE SURVEY

The Employee Satisfaction Survey (ESS) is the third and final TDS component.

We recommend that it be administered anonymously on an annual basis. The organization can determine which questions/issues the survey will cover, but most of our clients use a standard survey format we've developed—one which models a national standard for the best places to work—and cover a wide variety of important and integrated organizational issues.

(Sample ESS Questions)

(Sample ESS Summary Grid Report)

The survey again is anonymous, administered online by a third party (Team Excellence), and the results are available online. We recommend that administrators implement the ESS system in the following order and manner:

1. Determine ESS content (example survey content will be provided by Team Excellence).

2. Setup discrete and confidential online ESS account.

3. Determine ESS deployment schedule and duration.

4. Send organizational-wide announcement regarding implementation and deployment of ESS that reminds staff of the organization's accountability within the Team Covenant and provide outline of projected roll-out steps, timetable, and schedule (suggested draft will be provided).

5. Deploy ESS according to announced schedule.

6. Monitor ESS participation and send organizational-wide follow-up and reminder announcements as needed.

7. Within three to four weeks of ESS completion, senior leadership should meet as needed to review survey results, determine what specific actions the organization will take in direct response to the

survey feedback. Determine what additional action has merit, but is not feasible at the present time.

8. Determine what suggested action from the feedback it chooses not to take.

9. Within four to six weeks of ESS completion, the organization should publish the entire results of ESS along with a report on what action the organization's leadership has decided to take in direct response to the survey feedback, what action it cannot take, and what action it chooses not to take. A copy of this publication and report should be distributed to each employee and manager within the organization.

10. Following the distribution of the ESS survey results and the determined actions, department or small group meetings should be scheduled and conducted by one or more representatives of senior leadership to allow employees and managers to ask questions, discuss the results of ESS further, and build further trust within the organization as a result of ESS, providing employees a voice that senior leadership both hears and respects.

11. Consider optional use of ESS online suggestion box as routine opportunity for employees to offer anonymous suggestions on organizational improvement.

12. Use routinely regular staff meetings, employee newsletters, or other internal communication devices to focus on the organization's full completion and ongoing application of the total TDS system and the Team Covenant. The more attention and focus placed on honoring the commitments of TDS and the Team Covenant, the more positive influence the results this process will have on expediting the development of the organizational culture TDS is intended to help organizations achieve and sustain. Repetition is key.

13. Place ongoing high priority on ensuring that the various tools and components of TDS do not become just periodic or ritualistic organizational events, but become a continuous process of performance management focused on continuous improvement and professional growth by every individual within the organization.

Can you get voluntary participation? Yes. A voluntary participation rate of 35 percent to 50 percent is good and even considered high for a voluntary response to traditional employee surveys. However, we consistently receive response rates of 85 percent or higher (sometimes 100 percent participation) from our client's employees. The initial survey is taken twelve to fifteen months into implementation of the TDS and has been taught and sold during that period as formally representing the employee's voice. This "positioning" has a great deal to do with the level of participation we normally get. The ESS then becomes an annual process.

SAMPLE ESS
ANNOUNCEMENT E-MAIL

Subject: Annual Employee Satisfaction Survey (ESS)

From: Organization's CEO

As part of our organization's commitment to the Team Development Strategy and its Team Covenant, we conduct an annual Employee Satisfaction Survey. This survey is totally anonymous and is your opportunity, as an employee, to have a voice in the management and overall decision making of our business. Your response to the survey is an important component of our total commitment to accountability, and ESS is the process by which all employees hold the company and its leadership accountable for honoring the responsibilities outlined within the Team Covenant.

Please assume your Team Covenant responsibility by taking the few minutes required to complete this year's survey. Your participation is important and appreciated. The results of the survey and the decisions we make in how to appropriately respond to your voice will be presented to the entire staff upon completion of this year's ESS. Thank you in advance for your contributions, participation, and support of this very important component of our Team Development Strategy.

THE ORGANIZATION'S
REPORT CARD

Senior leadership must respond to its "report card." Remember, PSI is the tool the employees use to hold themselves and fellow employees accountable to the TC and for their performance; PARS is the tool the organization uses to hold employees accountable, and ESS is the tool employees use to hold the organization accountable.

Senior leadership must honor the agreement and complete the full circle of accountability. Not doing this destroys the credibility of the TDS and the TC, and makes the whole process exactly what companies traditionally achieve with it—a platitude to hang on the wall.

I have a colleague who was once a department head at a New York-based marketing communications firm. Small and dynamic, the company was a leader in its field because the CEO, who we'll call Kendall, was fanatical about finding the right people for the right jobs and conducting performance reviews twice a year. There was no psychometric testing, however, since Kendall considered himself a good judge of character. Although his employees sometimes debated this self-assessed "performance competency," they couldn't argue with the fact that the company was a great place to work, and that they functioned well as a team.

In the early 1990s, the firm experienced rapid growth as a result of Kendall's habit of promising prospective clients nearly anything they wanted without first consulting the staff members responsible for fulfilling the promises. As a result, the workloads of the creative and accountable personnel were skyrocketing, and "little details" were beginning to "slip through the cracks." In response, the company launched an employee survey to solicit feedback on everyone's perceived problems as well as suggestions for improvement.

Unfortunately, most of the suggestions and feedback were ignored, and a new account manager was hired to act as liaison between Kendall (salesman-in-chief) and the people responsible for actually developing and implementing marketing and PR strategies. Worse, this new liaison turned out to be a disaster—a drug user with various emotional problems. By relying solely on the new hire to manage client expectations and relationships, Kendall placed a virtual iceberg in the path of his "Titanic." Within four months of the employee survey and three months of the new liaison's start date, the company lost several key clients, and Kendall had to lay off most of his staff.

The lesson here is that the ESS requires management to walk the talk. The ESS should never be used as a clichéd "suggestion box" method for placating the unruly masses until the heat is off. ESS is the leadership's and management's report card.

To reinforce what I outlined earlier, we recommend to all our clients that within forty-five days of the survey's completion, they take the following steps:

- Senior management meets (as often as necessary) to review the feedback and suggestions of employees and determine what response it will give to the entire ESS report.

- Produce and distribute to every employee a document (typically a booklet) which spells out what management's response will be to the survey—including specific steps that management will take in response to suggested issues, as well as those things management cannot do anything about or "respectfully" disagrees with and chooses not to do anything about.

- Schedule a meeting or series of meetings during which management will meet with employees to discuss the report and answer any questions (a fireside chat approach).

- Create a virtual suggestion box. The ESS provides a secondary survey option for clients to use. It is a totally anonymous process that allows employees to access a 24/7/365 survey to input any issues, concerns, complaints, or (preferably) suggestions for improvement to management. Clients can then run reports at will, typically once a month, that are provided within this electronic or virtual suggestion box process.

THE IMPORTANCE OF
EXIT INTERVIEWS

When employees voluntarily leave the company, it provides an important opportunity to obtain information, from their perspective, on why they chose to leave, what the company does well, what the company needs to improve or change, etc. Exit interviews provide management with feedback they do not want to miss if they are serious about their commitment to the TC and want to maximize the ongoing organizational development process. We can provide clients with third party–administered (more objective and less intimidating) exit interview capability.

Most importantly, the feedback gleaned during exit interviews can prove invaluable in helping to reduce voluntary employee turnover, as noted in the SHRM white paper:

Some voluntary turnover is avoidable and some is unavoidable. Avoidable turnover stems from causes that the organization may be able to influence. For example, if employees are leaving because of low job satisfaction, the company could improve the situation by redesigning jobs to offer more challenge or more opportunities for people to develop their skills. Unavoidable turnover stems from causes over which the organization has little or no control. For instance, if employees leave because of health problems or a desire to return to school, there may be little the organization can do to keep them.

The distinction between avoidable and unavoidable turnovers is important because it makes little sense for a firm to invest heavily in reducing turnover that arises from largely unavoidable reasons. However, the line between avoidable and unavoidable turnover can be fuzzy. . .

Through surveys and exit interviews, organizations can identify the percentage of people leaving who follow each of the four primary paths to turnover: [dissatisfaction, better alternatives; personal/professional plans that conflict with the employment; shocks and/or emergencies that prompt/compel the employee to leave the organization]. Each path has different implications for the company's retention strategies.

HONORING THE CONTRACT

The impact and effectiveness of the TDS are entirely dependent on a proven and sustained commitment that "walks the talk" with the Covenant. "Yeah, I've heard all that before," is the common refrain from most employees when they first hear about our process. It's a "proof is in the pudding" phenomenon that takes at least a year (or longer) for our system to gain credibility. So again, when prospects or new clients ask how long the process is going to take, we respond "three to four years," because that much time is necessary to build trust and credibility in the overall system. It is also the time needed to gain skills and experience in the application of the system. All of the following require time to implement and honor:

- Gaining experience in the use of PSI and PARS (both managers and employees).

- Learning the language of PSI.

- Learning how to maintain an open and ongoing coaching dialogue between a manager and employee.

- Changing the culture's approach to making mistakes.

- Encouraging accomplishments.

- Rewarding success.

- Keeping communications open and specific.

Sounds like this is a great place to work! We've come full circle to my earlier point that if employees don't like what they're doing, they won't find satisfaction in their jobs and cannot possibly do those jobs well. We also return to my points about the very premise of the Team Covenant, as well as Daniel Pink's three keys to motivating others—autonomy, mastery, and purpose. All of these things build on each other to create a culture of energy and momentum where employees recognize your organization as the best place they've ever worked. Their sense of satisfaction and personal ownership is what reduces turnover, lowers operating costs and improves productivity and performance, and why the Team Development Strategy works—as a metrics-driven, bottom-line oriented process and not a touchy feely approach.

Ultimately, we must all recognize the simple truism that managers must treat employees with decency and vice versa. Relationships are a two-way street where the "Golden Rule" is both obvious and operable. That's the model. That's the Team Covenant. It is the living, breathing embodiment of all those plaques hanging on the walls of corporate lobbies, but only when it is put into the hands of leaders with belief, conviction, and courage.

Kendall (from our previous example) may have intellectually acknowledged the necessity of all this, but more than likely, he would never live up to it through his own behavior because he didn't truly believe that accountability is a two-way street. One of the things that I'm trying to give managers is permission to fulfill the promises of the Team Covenant and TDS as legitimate business tools. I'm giving you permission and encouragement to jump on the bandwagon of the Team Covenant.

When I tell people what I'm telling you right now, they say, "Yes!" When I know what you do (PARS), and why you do it your way (PSI), then I can affect your performance, I can coach, I can mentor, I can help you, and you can assume responsibility at your own level of accountability for improving what you do in ways you could never do without those two pieces of information being integrated. And that's why this system works. I find it hard to believe that no one has ever integrated these tools before.

One reason is because there are many people with too many territorial silos protecting their piece of the pie. They already have the tools but they think, *Well, personality testing for team building is something we do over in the training and development department. Performance assessment is something totally different, so we'll do that in the professional services group.*

Every successful organization adds up to more than the sum of its parts, which is why "silo thinking" is both unproductive and often dangerously shortsighted thinking. The TC and TDS are collectively Public Enemy #1 to silo thinking. They represent the kind of holistic thinking needed for the successful twenty-first-century company.

Chapter 8
MOVING FORWARD

THE LEARNING
ARC OF THE COVENANT

We have a client that's making serious progress applying the TDS, but has a major stumbling block with one of its senior executives. He's a classic old-school thinker who represents the "autocratic compliance" mentality as much as anyone I've ever met. Although he professes to subscribe to the TDS and the Covenant, his behavior continuously contradicts that alleged belief.

I thought he would cause the process to stall indefinitely, but after several years into the project, the organization has figured him out. Everyone wishes he would change, but he won't. He believes that "this is my company, and the rules for everyone else don't apply to me." Fortunately, there is enough consistent support and participation from the remaining senior leadership that the TDS is sustaining its credibility with the employees, and the organization is making measurable progress. However, this individual has slowed the success of the process by one or two years, and it's been an expensive lesson for the client. As I've said before, the success of the TDS depends on the genuine belief, commitment, and participation of senior leadership.

When working with another client, we confronted a thirty-year veteran of the organization—a senior manager and head of operations.

While the owner was totally committed to the Covenant and TDS, the operations manager represented a major stumbling block. In this situation, the company was faster to realize that this individual didn't "get it," and didn't *want* to "get it," so he had to be terminated. An exit strategy with a generous financial package was developed, and the senior manager was informed of his fate.

I've never seen anyone more surprised or more panicked. He literally begged and even showed some out-of-character emotion for a guy whose reputation was a demanding autocrat. He protested loudly and gave assurances that he'd experienced a "come to Jesus" epiphany and would now get on board.

But the owner knew this wouldn't happen. Still, the owner places high value on individual loyalty, so he eventually allowed this veteran to assume a consulting role during a year of transition, where he played a productive role in developing a documented process for company operations and a detailed operations manual. After that, he took his generous separation/retirement package.

The moral of these two tales is adapt or perish. Any organization that is committed to the beliefs that support the TC and TDS and wants to implement the business process in the most cost- and time-efficient manner possible, will likely experience some personnel "casualties"—voluntary and involuntary. Although most employees would rather work in an environment where compensation is directly related to job performance, where achievements are awarded, and where their opinions are heard and treated with respect, not everyone will buy-in. In many large organizations especially, there are always some employees who have become expert at "flying under the radar"—doing *just* enough to avoid getting fired. And within these companies, one or more managers will refuse to accept that "old school" is out... forever.

Historically, most die-hard autocrats don't *willingly* submit to calls for constitutional democracy without a fight. Some would rather die than grant more ownership accountabilities and rewards to "underlings"—the very people who used to say "How high, sir!" whenever this leader asked them to jump. I sometimes feel sorry for these recalcitrant managers, and we certainly give them every opportunity to learn and adapt to the new system. But when these people become an immovable obstacle, they must be removed. I typically tell prospective clients that not everyone will cross the finish line. That's only fair.

This can be one of the hardest steps for management to take. It's sometimes a deal killer—especially when the personnel obstacles are at the top of the "food chain." But it's something that must be done if the organization hopes to achieve success. That's because *the Team Covenant and Team Development Strategy are not compatible with old school ways and beliefs.* These two "ideologies" and business systems are as diametrically opposed to one another as free market capitalism and communism. *And they definitely cannot coexist within the same organization.*

For many people, particularly members of the emerging workforce, the TC and TDS make perfect sense and are a natural fit. These younger workers expect nothing less from their companies and leaders. For many older managers and employees, however, the system requires a significant investment in learning new processes and new ways of communicating. There is a significant "learning arc for the Team Covenant—one that requires people to adopt new communication habits and systems based on precedents with which they may not be familiar (or in love with).

Communication is both a set of skills and a process. The TDS applies a step-by-step process of defining information, sharing information, and establishing a pattern of repetitive feedback relative to results. The Team Covenant sets in motion a number of standards in *what* and *how* communication is to take place. For most organizations, it often raises the bar on what those standards should be, particularly in the interpersonal arena.

When our clients build a communication routine around the TC, TDS, PSI, PARS, and ESS, they develop better habits and expectations for communicating one-on-one, and as teams, departments, and organization-wide. These improved habits and expectations transfer into all the other forms and processes of communication that occur within the organization. It's akin to someone learning new manners; you learn to treat everyone better—not just the person teaching you the new manners. From there, these *new manners* are woven into the organizational fabric and culture.

I know I've "harped" on this point repeatedly, but that's because I can't emphasize it strongly enough: Regardless of what every manager says when first presented with the concepts covered in this book—and almost everyone nods in agreement or professes that he's been "converted"—senior leadership *must* sincerely believe in the philosophy of the TC and TDS and fully commit to implementing this system to have any hope of succeeding. Like the "Ark of the Covenant" in *Raiders of the Lost Ark*, the

Team Covenant is a source of almost "miraculous power" in the hands of enlightened managers and leaders, and when it is applied for the right reasons.

But when the very leaders who profess belief in the Covenant merely feign commitment or employ the system as a public relations dodge, the results can be disastrous. No, this "learning arc" won't melt the faces off your senior managers, but it may well prompt the "meltdown" of your traditional "compliance" culture without substituting something better in its place.

SERVANT LEADERSHIP

Generally speaking, the most effective leaders are somewhat visionary. They understand that part of their role is "pointing people toward the future" and inspiring them to embrace it with enthusiasm. There is a movement afoot called "servant leadership," which holds that the modern leader understands that every employee is his customer. (The traditionalist is concerned only with external customers.)

I tread this ground lightly and with a bit of trepidation. I think the "servant leader" concept is a good one, but it's an even more delicate subject than the "Covenant concept." But the fact remains that servant leaders, who see their role as providing the resources, support, and top-down empowerment to their employees, are pretty darned enlightened and more appealing to the emerging workforce than the traditional compliance leaders. Most leaders still don't possess "servant leader" strengths in quantity, but most of the leaders who manage successful organizations already display a combination of interpersonal awareness and tactical finesse. So it's not much of a stretch from where they are today to servant leadership.

BEYOND PERFORMANCE
MANAGEMENT

It's important to note that the TC and TDS are continuing to evolve. There are probably some applications we haven't yet considered, as well as some we are only beginning to investigate. One application that we are currently considering is using the PSI as a standard component in the job interview/screening process.

Though I don't believe that candidates should be hired solely on the basis of the PSI results, the surveys could (and maybe should) become part of the interviewing process. Instead of reading fifty résumés and narrowing the short list to ten, and then narrowing the list further—to five or three or two—BEFORE running a psychological profile, HR directors and managers could FIRST conduct the surveys with all fifty job candidates. Organizations could use this tool from the very start and, at the end of the process, give the other forty-nine candidates free career-planning advice based on the results. This would build great goodwill with an enhanced brand for the company, especially because the "losing" candidates would continue to have access to the Team Excellence website and its online training support. Everybody wins!

Organizations could announce to every new job applicant that, "We are a Team Covenant company. We'll give you the PSI results whether you come to work for us or not. You're going to learn and grow from our interviewing process." Nobody's doing that right now. Nobody – except some of our clients.

It makes complete sense to create a short list of candidates based on consideration of PSI results. It makes complete sense to determine if a job applicant represents a "match made in heaven or in hell" based on his/her PSI report and those of the team members with whom he/she would be working. The applicant may be a great salesperson or a great accountant. But the $64,000 question then becomes, "Is she going to be a great fit with this organization and especially with her managers, direct reports, colleagues, and subordinates? Is it likely that she will quickly and effortlessly adapt to our culture, or will she resist that culture, or even try to flout it?"

When a candidate comes in to be interviewed, he will receive feedback about his PSI as a way of initiating a conversation that goes something like this, "It looks like your strengths are in X, Y, and Z, but it's possible that you'll need to shore up your performance competencies in A, B, and C." Before he is even hired, the managers who are next in line to interview this person will be given PSI information about the candidate, AND the person being interviewed will be given PSI information about the people for whom (and with whom) he'll be working.

When have you ever gone for a job interview and been given psychological profile information about the people you'd be working with? My guess is never. That's why we are unique. We're on a mission to change the world!

As a job candidate who fits into the "Thinker" quadrant, wouldn't you want to *know* if four out of five of your supervisors scored heavily in the blue (Doer) or Orange (Counter) quadrant? If it were me, I'd immediately question whether I'd be a good match for this team. On a bad "hair day," most of my bosses would demand that I follow these rules and those rules "because they said so" (hopefully overstated), while I'd be continuously questioning the value of the rules and even rebelling whenever I thought I could get away with it.

Can you imagine how useful this information would be? Think how empowering it would be for all of the parties involved?

Imagine the first impression your organization would make on members of the emerging workforce when your HR director tells them that you really "walk the talk" when it comes to the TC and TDS and then outlines the processes and procedures you have put in place to reward outstanding performance, hold managers, employees, and the organization accountable for coaching, mentoring, open communication, and continuous performance improvement?

If I were a job candidate, my eyes would bug out. "Wow! You mean this company *actually* puts its money where its wall plaques are?"

Imagine what would happen if every new candidate were given a copy of the Team Covenant before he filled out the job application?

THAT is good public relations.

THAT would impress me.

When this sort of procedure is installed within an organization, it creates instant and lasting credibility. Who wouldn't want to work for a company where strengths are recognized and rewarded? There's a reason everyone has different strengths, and it's time that personal work preferences and styles were appreciated—not typecast as either "good or bad." There is no objective and universal good or bad when it comes to PSI results. There are strengths and areas that may require improvement in the context of the individual's job, the team, and the organization as a whole. It's not that X is good and Y is bad. It's about determining how to match X with Y—learning how to use these strengths to complement each other and get more done.

Would you want a company staffed only with blue personalities? You might get stuck with an organization where everyone demands that everybody else perform their tasks *his* way, or hit the highway. Conversely, an organization staffed entirely by orange or green preferences might be run like the Department of Motor Vehicles on the one hand, or like an enormous focus group on the other—one in which every employee had the power to veto any initiative she didn't like.

Beyond all this, we are working hard to develop new online tools to provide dynamic interactive dashboard reports for both individuals and teams. This capability will give individuals and managers on-demand options that allow them to study comparative information in a variety of formats and applications. In addition, we have an exciting, rather lengthy list of new, yet-to-be-developed reports. There is a great deal of important information in our database still to be *mined* and shared with clients.

CONSEQUENCES, NOT PUNISHMENT

One of the chief worries among some employees when they're first introduced to the TC and TDS is that the system will be used as a form of punishment for noncompliance. Obviously, this is the very opposite of what our system is designed to achieve. Under our process, accountability produces consequences (of course), but these consequences don't take the form of punishment—not unless the individual manager or employee refuses to honestly and sincerely participate in the goal of performance improvement.

One key point that I want to drive home is that the TDS and the TC put ultimate responsibility for accountability and success on the individual.

This is where it belongs, and our experience supports the fact that most successful companies are organizations in which every employee assumes a sense of ownership for the business's success. They are organizations in which employees have a clear understanding of how and where they contribute to profitability and growth.

At Team Excellence we do not design compensation programs, but we DO encourage clients to develop merit-based compensation systems with the following caveat. I strongly recommend that you *do not* directly tie compensation decisions to your implementation of PARS. In other words, do not devise a formula that says, "In order to receive X salary increase, you must obtain a score of Y on your PARS evaluation."

Instead, managers should use PARS as one of many factors that influence decisions about an employee's compensation adjustment. Managers need to learn to use good and all-encompassing judgment, rather than let one tool or set of data become a "crutch" to relieve them of their obligations to think and use good judgment.

This approach is one reason why our clients have enjoyed success with the Team Development Strategy as a whole. Using annual performance appraisal solely for the purpose of rationalizing compensation decisions is the main reason that traditional performance appraisals do not work. When compensation is the main purpose, performance appraisal systems become a political game, and they don't do much to improve performance. Instead, they're frequently used to justify decisions that were already made before the evaluation ever took place.

The "us/they" barrier that is so common to old school organizations has a lot of "punishment" expectations built into it. When the Team Covenant is honored, the ultimate outcome is that employees experience the consequences of their actions but not (in most cases) sanctions. PARS is a self-correcting system under which employee performance is objectively measured and *rewarded* when successful. When performance is *not* successful, it simply isn't rewarded. Traditional "carrots" are still offered to employees who measure up, but no sticks are applied to the backside, because none are needed. The "stick," in this instance, is the *absence* of rewards.

To us, this is very straightforward and logical, but many organizations have never used this approach. And in some cultures, it's not politically correct to withhold the trophies from the kiddies just because they didn't win. "We'll just assume they gave it their best shot, even though they preferred to sit on the bench and text message their friends."

Bottom line: If companies want accountability, they have to reward success and allow the natural order of things to occur when there's a lack of success, meaning consequences will ensue, but not punishment.

Reward success and good performance. Entrepreneurs will understand, appreciate and subscribe to this notion. Some unions and employees will not.

Do I believe in merit-based compensation systems? Yes.

Do we design them? No.

But I strongly believe in free enterprise, and I believe that people are more motivated to achieve success when they are given incentives and rewards. In my estimation, the absence of positive incentives and tangible rewards was a key factor in the collapse of the communist and other non-free-market economies.

The irony is that Karl Marx and Friedrich Engels might be considered astute analysts of nineteenth-century capitalism and its flaws. Unfortunately, their cures were worse than the "disease," thanks to the poorly drawn system of entitlement they proposed. Rather than giving everyone equal opportunity to excel and achieve their personal and professional goals and purposes, they made the same mistake that many of today's professed capitalists are making—*treating* everyone equally instead of providing equal opportunities for growth and development. (In another life, I might have allowed Marx to help model the Employee Satisfaction Survey, but I wouldn't have let him *near* the PSI, PARS, TC, and TDS.)

TEAMWORK VS. INDIVIDUALITY

The name of my company is "Team Excellence," and not "I'm Excellent."

I believe in teams.

If you talk to most managers, teambuilding and communication are often the priorities they mention first when talking about what they need to improve. Today, there is a greater acceptance of and awareness about the need to develop teams and get employees to buy in on the "team approach."

However, in keeping with the old adage that "a chain is only as strong as its weakest link," a team is only as affective as the capabilities of the individual members. That's why the Team Covenant was designed to focus on the responsibilities and accountabilities of the individual.

Strong, effective, and successful teams must recognize the importance of respecting the individuality of each member. The odds for success can be significantly enhanced if there is a neutral, nonjudgmental process to define that individuality. PSI provides that neutral, nonjudgmental language. It's an evaluation mechanism focused on strengths and interests. Therefore, it's a handy tool for identifying the inherent collaborative capabilities that every individual can bring to the team.

Teams don't just happen because people are designated to be members of the team. Teams need to be developed via the Team Development Strategy!

The Covenant states, "We agree to the best of our ability and within the limits of our resources to reward each employee commensurate with their motivation and performance and provide incentives for doing a job well. In return, we expect that each employee will constantly attempt to do their very best, show a desire for innovative growth and personal improvement, and strive to be excellent in all that they do."

Companies that understand this and mean this achieve remarkable performance from their employees. Southwest Airlines and Whole Foods are great examples. If you are unfamiliar with these two companies and their approaches, you might Google each one regarding their HR strategies and human capital success stories.

BE MORE THAN A BOSS!

Please be more than a boss! I challenge you to get out of the box and consider ways to become a better, more successful, and different kind of boss than you've been in the past. Through the process covered in this book, you have a tool for creating a more productive way to manage people and lead organizations. It may require more innovation and self-aware behavior on the parts of owners and leaders.

And it may require some risk-taking. It may also require a philosophic realignment. It will require a lot, but the rewards are increased when you embrace the TDS and become more than just a traditional boss. As much as anything, it requires relationship training and development that will probably stretch the abilities of many bosses.

THE OUTCOMES AT AZ-TECH

Overall, the TDS has been a major success for AZ-Tech, helping to reduce turnover and increase retention throughout most of the company's locations. While the industry turnover average exceeds 25 percent, AZ-Tech's average is now below 10 percent. At several locations, the average is higher, due to factors that include local market conditions and the level of support for the TDS among management. Turnover rates correlate to the annual results, by location, of the ESS. (The ESS is a reliable predictor *and* a tracking system for these important metrics.) Colin and the senior team pay continuous attention to this costly organizational issue, since the replacement costs for highly qualified professionals often equal two times each person's annual salary and benefits.

Today, more than 80 percent of employees rate AZ-Tech as an outstanding place to work, and say that they expect to work for the company for at least three years (or more). All of this translates into millions of dollars in annual cost savings and contributions to the bottom line. Conservatively, AZ-Tech is saving $25 million to $30 million per year in reduced turnover costs, compared to industry averages.

PSI has become an important management and coaching tool by providing a common language to managers and employees—a "lingua franca that allows everyone to communicate and collaborate more effectively *and* hold everyone accountable for the relational performance expectations of the Covenant. At AZ-Tech, it's become a fairly standard experience for the PSI to give individuals *permission* to be who they are, while providing them with the *tolerance* and *appreciation* for everyone's individual differences necessary to live out the Covenant. Realistically, there are exceptions. Some employees struggle to fully accept "other people's way of doing things" as okay when those ways are different from their own. But managers and teams are sincerely trying to develop better habits and skills when it comes to correcting and modeling appropriate behavior standards for those who fall short of the mark.

PSI is used openly and freely throughout the company to compare employee styles and approaches and to build stronger teams with less competition and conflict. The results are creating greater appreciation for building consensus and increasing individual and team productivity. PSI is used routinely to introduce new team members to their departments and work environments. And it is used throughout the hiring process to improve the interviewing of candidates and share with these candidates the PSI profiles of their prospective managers and work team colleagues. This gives candidates the unique ability to interview the company while being interviewed themselves. As a result, PSI has become a *very strong* selling point for the company among job candidates. Even those who are not hired walk away from their interview experience with an extraordinary appreciation of AZ's organizational culture.

PARS is an evolving success. Compared to years past, employees have much more objective and current information about specific performance goals and how they are doing in accomplishing those goals. This is especially true in departments and locations where managers use PARS as an ongoing platform to coach and develop continuous improved performance with their employees, rather than using PARS as merely an annual "how much more do you get paid" event. The system is intended to create an open-ended dialogue for continuous performance improvement, a stipulation of the Covenant. Some managers do better than others, but overall, goal-oriented performance has noticeably increased throughout the company.

Admittedly, it typically takes individual departments and branches eighteen to twenty-four months to properly learn the system and implement it with consistently successful outcomes. Senior management (appropriately and routinely) puts high-priority focus on the need for ongoing training, which includes training senior leadership to support and reinforce the system. They've learned from experience that the TDS cannot run on auto pilot.

Kelly Anderson in marketing and Gary Monroe in product development have become the most vocal proponents of TDS as well as the overall organizational development system. This is reflected in the success of their departments and functions, which include the lowest turnover rates in the company and the highest levels of achievement of business plan objectives.

Frank Girardi in operations has become a stronger TDS leader, though his area of responsibility has had more challenges in "walking the talk" consistently. Frank occasionally grumbles about having to "wet-nurse the screwups," but the external face that he presents to his employees is kinder, gentler, and more tolerant than before. The rest of the senior team work hard to support and encourage him, and he's come a long way. But there's a lot more room to grow.

Cheryl Bergen is the greatest champion of TDS and all of its components. HR has grown in both capability and stature at the senior table. She's worked tirelessly to develop her staff to support the implementation and ongoing administration of TDS. Cheryl and her staff have gained a significant amount of trust and confidence from the entire company, thanks to their commitment, support, and mastery of TDS. She has become a real player, basking in a newfound sense of personal and professional achievement. TDS gave her a vehicle for becoming a recognized leader and a "hero."

Colin Hathaway, like all leaders, has his good and bad hair days. Overall, he is very satisfied with the results the TDS has provided, and he sees the system as a major component of his leadership legacy. There are times when market conditions, financial challenges, or internal disagreements on how things should get done cause him to fall back on a few old behaviors, but in the grander scheme, he's become a very credible champion of TDS, and the company believes in his very genuine commitment.

Colin represents the most critical factor in the overall success of the TDS. Frankly, size does matter. The larger the organization, the harder it is to achieve sustained success through the TDS, because it takes sincere and relentless commitment and involvement on the part of the organization's senior leadership. Anything short of that will limit the degree to which TDS can contribute to the organization's performance management success. TDS requires a company's CEO to serve as a highly visible and engaged champion, one who requires the genuine buy-in and participation of his entire senior team. That is obviously easier to achieve in a smaller organization, but as Colin demonstrates, very feasible in larger organizations that are willing to take TDS seriously, and make the necessary commitment, *especially the commitment of time.*

Like any organizational strategy, TDS is a work in progress—one that recognizes room for ever-continuing growth and improvement, since human performance and behavior is a complex process that requires constant attention and leadership. The TDS is a process, not a panacea. It's a process that puts in place a system for continuous organizational development, keeping in mind that it lays the necessary foundation for performance accountability in *every* direction. Today, the emerging workforce is eager for accountability, and it rejects compliance as an acceptable approach to work and career.

Chapter 9
TWENTY-FIRST-CENTURY SKILLS

REAL TEAMWORK IS THE TREND

I once got a call from out of the blue, asking me to troubleshoot a project in Brazil. I'm not entirely sure why the company called me, other than sheer desperation, but this large engineering and construction company (specializing in electrical power plants) made me an offer I couldn't refuse.

My prospective client had been hired by a major energy production company, which we'll call Rio Bravo, to build an electric generation plant north of Rio de Janeiro. Since Rio didn't have adequate electricity at the time, civil unrest was beginning to occur, prompting the president of Brazil to take a personal interest in the project. The president was pressuring Rio Bravo, which pressured my client, demanding to know "When?"

Unfortunately, the answer to "When?" had become "Who knows?" Construction of the new power plant had come to a screeching halt.

My assignment was to fly to Brazil and resolve the conflict between my prospective client and Rio Bravo—to break the logjam and get the project back on track. It seemed like a nightmare to me since I was *really* not interested in working with two camps of old school thinkers.

To be candid, I didn't think this assignment would enhance my reputation—to put it mildly. I thought this was a lose-lose proposition. Because of its high-profile nature, my gut told me that this was an assignment I should decline. But instead of just saying "no," I decided to be "clever," making the conditions for acceptance so preposterous that the prospective client would tell me to "get lost." So I tripled my fees—literally tripled my fees—and made some other "movie-star-type" demands.

Instead, they accepted my offer.

I spent my first four days in Brazil meeting with my client's senior managers, discussing their views on what the problems were. I next met with the local senior management of Rio Bravo. Each group offered up "the usual suspects" for the delays, with one major exception: they both claimed that the biggest problems were being caused by the Brazilian subcontractors.

I said, "Okay, I want the top six or seven people from your organization, I want the top six or seven people from *your* organization, and *then* I want the top six to ten subcontractors to meet in a controlled, off-site environment. We will encamp there for the duration, and we won't leave until these issues are resolved."

We ended up on a private estate along the coast—in the little town of Buzios. (Buzios was an unknown village until discovered in the 1970s by Bridget Bardot, after which it became a jet-set enclave, with an annual jazz festival.) Anyway, the estate was turned over to us. The staff worked night and day for three days to prepare the place for our arrival, and we began. It was a very nice place.

The rule of engagement was this: the conference gets everyone's full and undivided attention until we find a resolution.

The discussions went on for days—ten to twelve hours per day—but in my judgment, we were getting nowhere. By the seventh morning, I was convinced this process was not going to succeed. I was actually preparing to acknowledge that and suggest that we admit our defeat. I was in the shower that seventh morning, doing some soul-searching and grasping for any tactic I hadn't yet tried.

Suddenly, a catchy little phrase popped into my mind.

We start our meeting at eight o'clock, and I said, "Gentlemen, I think I finally understand this. I know what the problem is. Whether or not you are willing to deal with it is really up to you." The two big company camps are Americans and Europeans, and they, of course, have been putting the blame all week long on these Brazilian subcontractors for not being up to task.

"I want you to look around. I want you to look at the creative, ingenious way in which this estate was converted—in less than three days—into a functional conference center. Pull up the tablecloths and look underneath."

And they did. We had plywood-assembled conference tables that had been made from nothing, because there had been no appropriate materials. I pointed out several other things that struck me as demonstrative of the creative, imaginative genius of the Brazilians who were hosting us—both in terms of the facilities and the service of the quickly assembled staff. I said, "So here's what it boils down to. If you're going to do business in Brazil, you've got to learn to samba." That was the phrase that had popped into my mind in the shower. Euphemistic, but they got it.

I was trying to say to them, "You're trying to build this power plant the way you would build it in America or in Germany, but you're in *Brazil*."

At this moment, the senior guy for the client said, "Can we take a break?"

"Of course, we can," I replied.

"Come with me," he said, motioning me out onto a balcony.

He continued once we were outside, "For the last six days, you've tried to sell us all of this psychological mumbo-jumbo—this philosophical bullshit of yours. I want you to look me in the eye, and tell me if you really in your heart and mind believe all of that crap, or if they're just your tricks of the trade."

I said, "I could not mean it more, or have more conviction and passion. I'm *that* genuine." Then I related a few war stories that I hadn't yet shared.

THEN, he said, *"I'm the problem, aren't I?"*

"Yes, sir. You are."

"I can fix this, can't I?"

"Yes, you can."

"Let's go," he said.

After we reentered the room, he walked to the front and said to me, "Come here." The moment I reached him at the front of the room, this tough, autocratic, super-blue-quadrant old-school son of a bitch put his arm around my shoulders. You have to understand that men in that industry don't touch each other. They just don't. But he put his arm around me and said, "We have a major problem here. This man was sent down here to try to help us, and I've come to believe that everything that he's been saying for the last six days is real. He's serious, he means it, he has great conviction, and we need to listen to him.

"I also believe that I'm the biggest obstacle in the path of this problem getting solved, so I want all of us to sit down and start talking more seriously than we have talked for the last week. I don't want us to leave until we've figured this thing out."

So we sat down and basically started all over again. We were there another five days, and we walked out of that conference with commitments and agreements and acknowledgments and a recognition that the Brazilians were doing the best they could and really had some good ideas that needed to be heard and taken seriously.

Four months later, the power plant was finished.

My client was happy. Rio Bravo was happy. The subcontractors were happy, and, most important, the president of Brazil was happy.

Rio de Janeiro was getting more electricity, and that was truly one of the great moments of my mission, my career, and my journey.

I've told this story, not just because it was a pivotal moment in my career, and one of the biggest inspirations for what would become the Team Covenant and the Team Development Strategy, but because the process that took place more than fifteen years ago reflects a process that is about to sweep away the old autocratic way of doing things.

Like it or not, increased—and genuine—teamwork, cooperation, and a more democratic way of conducting business are among the most important skills of the twenty-first-century business world. They're here to stay. Regardless of whether anyone pays attention, much less adopts, the principles and practices suggested in this book, the old way of doing things is dead, even if it hasn't been buried yet. To be profitable in the decades ahead, business must:

- Reduce the cost of achieving successful performance.
- Do a better job of defining the required results.
- Adjust to new employee expectations as well as career/life goals.

- Do a better job of engaging, motivating, and gaining commitments from individuals and teams.

- Provide equal opportunity without identical treatment.

- Become continuous coaching/mentoring organizations.

- Reward measured performance improvements.

- Most of all, dedicate the time and resources to making all of this happen.

Denial is not a strategy. Window dressing and wall plaques are not strategies.

The TC and TDS *are* proven, award-winning strategies that improve the bottom line. This process is not your father's "touchy-feely" drum circle, Kumbaya-singing consciousness-raising group, or a wall climbing/ trust exercise in team building at some mountain resort. It isn't something that's been relentlessly parodied in countless TV sitcoms and Hollywood movies. It's not some goofy fad.

It is *the* proven, tested, and award-winning performance management process designed to help management get more out of their human capital for less money. Today, we operate our businesses in a constantly changing environment that requires us to continuously adapt to new information and ideas. We must do a better job of sharing information and expectations throughout our organization that keeps all of us focused on the future, more than the past. The TC and TDS are proven and award-winning strategies that improve the bottom line.

It is also important that we define more specifically what we believe and why we are in business. We need to formally state our organizational philosophy to all of our employees and managers, ensuring that we place the right set of values on every individual as an important part of our total organization and the work we each do. Our success depends upon how well we define every employee's and manager's contribution to our organizational goals, how we measure results, how we provide continuous feedback, and how we hold everyone and the organization accountable.

We believe the Team Development Strategy offers a proven and practical solution to these challenges. How successful this new program becomes is dependent on each of us. We all must accept a new level of personal accountability, ownership, and entrepreneurial ownership, for the growth and continued success of our businesses.

Addendum
AN EPIPHANY ON OUR VALUE PROPOSTION

Since this book was first published, a lot has happened and we're very grateful for the reception *Team Covenant* has received and for the response by our clients in using this book as a text and training manual for their managers and employees to implement the Team Development Strategy.

Our client base has expanded and crossed additional oceans. In the last several years, our methodology and all three of our proprietary software tools have been translated into Mandarin, and TDS is now being introduced successfully in Mainland China as well as in Malaysia and Australia.

Many things, exciting things, are being demonstrated in all these new initiatives, but one fundamental truth remains the same, people are people. No matter who you are or where you come from, what we measure in our Personal Strengths Inventory (PSI) is universally the same. There are cultural trends, of course, but each day we validate that, all of us share the same humanity. PSI is proving again to be an easy-to-understand and nonjudgmental common language to define our individuality and build strong, trusting, and productive relationships.

And the contract of *Team Covenant* is working.

People and companies are recognizing that *Team Covenant* provides a formula and model for behavioral change at the individual, team, and organizational levels.

There is a great deal going on socially, economically, and politically in our country, as elsewhere. One very prominent issue where behavioral change may have as much significance as anywhere else is in the arena of healthcare and wellness. No other issue, short of the struggling economy as a whole, has captured more attention than the spiraling costs of healthcare. Figuring it out is on everyone's bucket list.

I take a pretty conservative stance on the issue of healthcare, especially from the business owner's perspective. But know that I genuinely respect those who disagree with me. Certainly, everyone wants and needs high-quality healthcare, and I truly don't want people going without the healthcare they need. But from a business perspective, I don't believe that healthcare is either a right or an entitlement. Rather, wellness is an organizational imperative and an individual responsibility. Unfortunately, the myriad of wellness programs popping up everywhere in companies today are simply not getting the job done.

There will be no wellness until people change their behavior. It's that simple.

Why, you may ask, am I raising the notion of wellness within the context of the Team Covenant and the Team Development Strategy? The answer again is quite simple. It's not to be opportunistic. Wellness in a variety of ways is vital to a Team Covenant work environment and culture. And wellness is much more than mere physical illness prevention or preventative care. Wellness in our view is as much, if not more, psychological wellness than it is physical wellness. It is after all, within the psychological realm of our lives that we experience (or do not experience) the most significant stresses.

As much as anything, it is stress that prevents us from achieving total or lasting wellness. Stress is the root cause of much of our physical maladies and limitations.

In both our personal and professional lives, conflict, misunderstanding, lack of trust, critical judgment of others, intolerance, anger, and other elements of our humanity (our individual differences) contribute to the absence of wellness. This is not to deny the importance of the physical issues like weight, diet, exercise, blood pressure, cardiology, vision, diabetes, and so on. But please rest assured that relational wellness, at home and at work, is as much a part of achieving total overall wellness as anything else. And the Team Covenant is all about relational wellness. TDS is certainly not a panacea, but it is a proven and successful organizational process.

Our role and contribution to organizational wellness is in helping to establish and nurture this thing we call relational wellness -- people and organizations engaging and holding one another accountable. We're privileged to work in partnership with our clients to facilitate the increased self- and interpersonal awareness that leads to individual accountability, organizational collaboration, and most important, genuine and lasting TRUST – relational wellness if you will. It has been and continues to be an amazing journey.

We are very grateful. Thank you.

THE TEAM COVENANT™

At our company, we are a team, and we recognize that our employees are truly our most valuable resource. Without a highly trained and motivated workforce, our company cannot possibly succeed and achieve our expectations. The leadership of this company is committed to providing a work environment where employees are given the opportunity to achieve their highest potential, while experiencing dignity, respect, and job satisfaction in the work we each perform.

We believe that the very best work outcomes are accomplished when all employees share a sense of mutual ownership for successful results, and where each employee accepts personal accountability for their individual contributions. These beliefs reflect our organizational philosophy, and this philosophy requires a constant focus and dedication to the following specific covenants.

*1. **WE AGREE** to treat all employees with courtesy and respect and to recognize the value of their individuality. We will strive to always give recognition when employees do their job well. When a job is not done well, we want to focus on "what" went wrong and "how" to correct it in the future and not lose sight of the individual employee's worth and value. This is how we demonstrate individual dignity and respect. In return, **WE EXPECT** that each employee will always try to do their very best, assume accountability for the work they perform, and continuously attempt to grow and improve in their job.*

2. WE AGREE to give all employees the right and the opportunity to express their individual points of view, to be heard, and to share in an open and honest dialogue about how we work together, without recrimination or fear of political consequences from within our organization. In return, WE EXPECT that each employee will always be honest, maintain total integrity, and express themselves in a courteous, mature, and professional manner with everyone at all times.

3. WE AGREE to the best of our ability and within the limits of our resources to reward each employee commensurate with their demonstrated motivation and performance and provide incentives for doing a job well. In return, WE EXPECT that each employee will constantly attempt to do their very best, show a desire for innovative growth and personal improvement, and strive to be excellent in all that they do.

4. WE AGREE to share information throughout our organization whenever possible and to keep every employee as well informed as we can. We understand the need, value, and importance of open communication, and we know that people perform at their best when they fully understand what is going on. In return, WE EXPECT each employee to communicate clearly, specifically, politely, and professionally with our company's management and fellow employees as we all work together.

5. WE AGREE to take the time necessary to accomplish this overall covenant. We live and work in a highly demanding world of work and acknowledge that time is a very difficult resource to manage. Training, organizational growth and development, and team building require time. In return, WE EXPECT each employee to assume the responsibility and be accountable for using time effectively and to apply themselves fully in their participation in the implementation of this overall covenant.

6. We genuinely believe in the "Golden Rule" as meaning treat others as you would like to be treated. This age-old guiding principle complements our organizational philosophy. WE AGREE to honor this rule with each employee, and in return, WE EXPECT each employee to demonstrate this rule toward others in the performance of their job.

This team covenant should guide our daily performance and behavior. If we accomplish this, we will continue to grow as an excellent and stable company that provides a secure and long-term career opportunity to every employee. Because we are people, we will make mistakes and may, unfortunately, sometimes fall short of our own self-determined expectations. If and when we do fall short of these expectations, we should acknowledge our mistakes, apologize for them, and sincerely promise to try harder and do better.

We are a service-driven organization with a strong sense of community. Therefore, this covenant among ourselves should extend first to each of our families, and then to our customers, suppliers, and all of the other professional relationships in which we engage. This will make us a very unique, strong, and effective team.

Once again, we want each employee to experience a pride of ownership in our business and our company's success. We believe that each member of our team must find satisfaction and enjoyment in the work they do for our company, if they are to maximize their job performance and personal career experience. This team covenant is an expression of our genuine commitment to this very important and essential goal and to the organizational culture we aspire to create and maintain.

As a team, let's move forward with excitement, optimism, and enthusiasm into the successful future we can all share together.

Name _____

Signature _____

BIBLIOGRAPHY

Allen, David G., Ph.D., SPHR. *Retaining Talent: A Guide to Analyzing and Managing Employee Turnover.* SHRM Foundation, 2008.

Confronting the coming talent crunch: What's next? 2006 Manpower White Paper.

Collison, J. *Future of the U.S. labor pool.* SHRM Research, 2005

Cascio, W. F. 2006. Managing Human Resources: Productivity, Quality of Work Life, Profits (7th ed). Burr Ridge, IL: Irwin/McGraw-Hill. Mitchell, T. R., Holtom, B. C., & Lee, T. W. 2001. How to Keep Your Best Employees: Developing an Effective Retention Policy. *Academy of Management Executive, 15,* 96–108.

Sommer, R. D. 2000. *Retaining intellectual capital in the 21st century.* SHRM White Paper.

Gallup Study: Feeling Good Matters in the Workplace. Gallup Management Journal news release, January 16, 2006.

Parker-Pope, Tara. "Time to Review Workplace Reviews?" *The New York Times,* May 17, 2010.

Kane, Tim. "Why Our Best Officers Are Leaving." *The Atlantic Monthly,* January/February 2011.

Culbert, Samuel. "Get Rid of the Performance Review!" *The New York Times,* March 1, 2011.

INDEX

ABOUT THE AUTHOR

Randy Hopkins is president and CEO of Team Excellence Inc., a Houston-based organizational development and management consulting firm specializing in performance management and leadership development. Team Excellence provides its clients with proprietary systems for personality and behavioral assessment, employee performance appraisal, strategic organizational assessment, and various other organizational feedback processes. Team Excellence has received two human resource industry awards for its unique metrics-driven system of organizational performance accountability called *the Team Development Strategy.*

Hopkins says above all else, Team Excellence is and has always been in the relationships business. He believes that building sustained and genuine trust and lasting relationships today, is really the name of the game.

Founded in 1980, Team Excellence's clients have represented a wide variety of businesses and industries and have included IBM, Xerox, Tenneco, Nabisco, NL Industries, Bechtel, CompleteRx, Merrill Lynch, Bank of America, Kraft Foods, BMC Software, Dynegy, Memorial Hospital System, Aker Kvaerner, Procter & Gamble, Hunt Oil, New Process Steel, Sterling Bank, Catholic Extension, MD Anderson Cancer Center, and Patriot Bank, among others.

Prior to founding Team Excellence, Randy began his career as the training and development manager for an operating division of Tenneco Inc. He later served as training manager for the Amerada Hess refinery on St. Croix in the U.S. Virgin Islands, and then joined the staff of an international psychological testing and consulting firm where he served as a senior associate and vice president.

Randy has spoken to professional organizations, conferences, and corporations in the United States, Latin America, and Europe about today's changing business environments, the evolving attitudes and expectations of employees, and a growing need to align organizational business objectives with the goals and individual career aspirations of employees. A major concern today, in his opinion, is the need for organizations to focus more attention on employee engagement and retention in order to improve performance and productivity and lower the excessive costs of employee turnover and talent replacement.

Throughout his career, Randy has been actively involved in professional and community organizations including the American Society for Training and Development, the American Society of Management Consultants, the National Speakers Association, the Texas Governor's Committee on Business and Education Development, and the American Institute of Banking Educational Advisory Board. Other community service includes lecturing on the management and behavioral sciences for several colleges and universities, as well as hosting a weekly televised broadcast on career issues for KHTV in Houston, Texas.

Randy and his wife, Carolyn, reside in Houston, Texas.

WHY SOME COMPANIES ARE BETTER TO WORK FOR THAN OTHERS

An Insider's Look at Performance Management as a Contractual Agreement Between Employees and Management Based Upon Building Trust, Relationships, and Accountability

ORDER COPIES TODAY

for Your Staff, Business, or Organization!

ORDER ONLINE: www.Xlibris.com

Also available at Amazon.com and Barnes & Noble.

Team Excellence Inc.
Phone: (281) 488-0935
E-mail: info@teamexcellence.com
www.teamexcellence.com

© 2011 Team Excellence, Inc.